epiphanies

*moments of grace
in daily life*

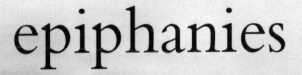

epiphanies

moments of grace
in daily life

mary murphy

VERITAS

First published 2007 by
Veritas Publications
7/8 Lower Abbey Street
Dublin 1
Ireland
Email publications@veritas.ie
Website www.veritas.ie

ISBN 978 1 85390 954 2

Lines from the poems below are quoted in this book. They have become so much a part of the author's vocabulary that she is unable to state exactly where she encountered them: p. 8, from 'Pied Beauty' by G.M. Hopkins; p. 9, from 'Snow' by Louis McNiece; p. 13, lines from Patrick Kavanagh; p. 38, from 'A Dialogue between the Soul and Body' by Andrew Marvell; p. 43, from 'The Darkling Thrush' by Thomas Hardy; p. 69, 'Death, be not Proud' by John Donne; p. 76, lines from J.C. Squires; p. 79, from 'The Flower' by George Herbert; p. 84, from 'Surprised by Joy' by William Wordsworth; p. 100, from 'Lucy Poems' by William Wordsworth; p. 111, from 'Easter Wings' by George Herbert; p. 115, 'Deniall' by George Herbert; p. 119, from 'The Hebridean Altars' by Alistair Maclean; p. 121, 'Prayer Finisterre' by Carol Ann Duffy.

Designed by Colette Dower
Printed in the Republic of Ireland by Betaprint, Dublin

Veritas books are printed on paper made from the wood pulp of managed forests. For every tree felled, at least one tree is planted, thereby renewing natural resources.

To the lights in my life:

Daithi, my husband and friend;

Niall, my dear, dear son;

Jan, my precious daughter-in-law;

Rianna, Matthew, Georgia,
my beautiful grandchildren.

Contents

Introduction

Twenty years ago or so, when Rev. Dr Bert Tosh (Senior Producer, Religious Programmes, BBC Northern Ireland) telephoned me to ask if I would be willing to contribute to BBC's *Thought for the Day* series, I remained uncharacteristically silent for several seconds before suggesting timidly that he might be confusing me with someone else: an eminent theologian, perhaps, or a person of extraordinarily high moral rectitude. 'No,' Rev. Bert replied cheerfully, 'you'll do! Just write out of your own experience and it'll be grand.'

I did as I was told and what followed over the years is mostly contained within the covers of this little book: thoughts wrought out of the stuff of my life, a very ordinary life; a life, no less, no more, touched by epiphanic moments than any other. These epiphanic moments, these moments of illumination, of clarification, of extraordinary showing forth, I have attempted to articulate, as they have informed my losses and my gains.

Although I have arranged the 'thoughts' in, more or less, chronological order, they certainly do not chart any kind of linear progression in spiritual wisdom; rather they often describe a 'one step forwards, two steps backwards' kind of progress. If this book reflects anything back at me, it is the image of an ordinary, flawed human being's attempt to articulate the transfiguring effects of God's grace; the reality of God's love.

A different kind of language

Language, in all its moods, registers and forms, fascinates me. It always has. Poetry, prose, song, debate: words weaving and dancing themselves into the shapes of the meanings of things. As a child, I learned the language of comfort and consolation from my mother; the language of song and story from my father. As an adult, a joy is an evening spent with friends who are willing to talk into the small hours of the morning.

All in all, I suppose it is no wonder that I ended up teaching language, attempting to excite young people about the wonder of words and the magical meanings that can be fashioned out of them. 'Listen!' I'd say. 'Listen to this.'

> Glory be to God for dappled things –
> For skies as couple-colour as a brindled cow;
> For rose-moles all in stipple upon trout that swim;
> Fresh-firecoal chestnut-falls; finches' wings;
> Landscape-plotted and pieced-fold, fallow, and plough;
> And all trades, their gear and tackle and trim.
>
> FROM 'PIED BEAUTY' BY G.M. HOPKINS

Or

The room was suddenly rich and the great bay-window
was
Spawning snow and pink roses against it
Soundlessly collateral and incompatible:
World is suddener than we fancy it.

World is crazier and more of it than we think,
Incorrigibly plural. I peel and portion
A tangerine and spit the pips and feel
The drunkenness of things being various.

FROM 'SNOW' BY LOUIS MCNIECE

'Language is your thing', people say to me – and, yes, I
suppose it is. Yet, I know there is a language I do not always
hear, a language not on my usual frequency, one that needs
my full and absolute consent before it becomes intelligible
to me; a language I can only listen to with my heart. It is
the language of God, a tongue I do not always understand;
one I have had to learn slowly and in stillness. It is the
language of faith, the language of the creative imagination,
of unselfishness, of true love. I can hear this language when
God speaks to me through the events of my daily life, when
my dreams are shattered, my hopes dashed, my best-laid
schemes frustrated. Gradually, please God, I will become
accustomed to his language and, through it, his ways and
his will. Someday, perhaps when I am most alone, with a
blinding clarity, I will know that God is not a stranger to
me, that I have finally learned his language and his words
will dance and weave themselves into the shapes of the
meaning of things.

Nourish the earth

Last month, on the kind of day she had loved so well, we laid our friend, Eileen, to rest. A small group of us huddled together a little apart from the other mourners – 'the gang'. We had grown up together, gone to school together, shared each other's clothes and dreams, laughed and anguished together. Eileen had been the gentlest of us. She was the music lover who played the piano like an angel; she had been baking feather-light cakes before the rest of us could boil an egg; she had been the first to marry, the first to be a mother – and she had welcomed each of her five children as a breathtaking miracle.

'I can't believe it,' one of us whispered through her tears. 'I can't believe it.' Afterwards, we walked out together – a sad little group. I knew the others were feeling as lost and as uncomprehending as I was. Intimations of mortality! 'In the early autumn of her life' was what the priest had said about Eileen. I shivered in the chilly air.

Before we parted, I looked deeply into the faces of my friends. Each face was etched here and there with tiny lines; each pair of eyes held secrets I had not shared. I was conscious for the first time of our separateness. Always before now, when we met, no matter how long it had been, we managed within minutes to become 'the gang' again; laughing as if we hadn't a care in the world, as if there wasn't a child or a husband or a mortgage to worry about. Now, as I looked into the faces of my friends, I grieved for all of us. Our circle was broken. Eileen was gone.

On the way home I did not offer to share the driving with my husband as I normally would. I knew I would make mistakes and maybe get us both killed. I had no faith in my judgement anymore, in my ability to control the wheel. I thought of our son away from home and in a rush of wild panic imagined him in terrible danger. Oh, why couldn't I gather my loved ones in one place, lock the doors and windows and keep them safe forever!

I phoned one of my friends that night, the one who likes to know we have arrived home safely.
'Why is Eileen dead?' I sobbed down the line. 'I can't bear it!'
'What matters is that Eileen lived,' came my friend's quiet reply. 'You know the way Eileen lived,' she continued, 'everything she did glowed. Remember her courage. She loved every single day of her life and everything it brought her. It's her having been alive that matters.'

The grip of terror on my heart began to loosen a little and I willed life to claim me again. Please God, I thought, let me live my life every day as Eileen lived hers: with love and courage. Let me nourish the small patch of earth you have given me so that it bears good fruit.

Shrinking

When I was a child and terrified at night by the thunderous heartbeat and ragged breathing of the invisible monster who lurked under my bed, I taught myself a trick to keep me safe: I shrank to the point of invisibility and then waited, barely breathing, ears and mouth stopped up, for the monster to leave quietly because there simply was no one there to gobble up for his supper.

Over the years I've sometimes caught myself out exercising the same trick again: for instance when media coverage of human suffering at the hands of other humans was too horrifying to contemplate, I'd shrink. I'd shrink before the catastrophic results of natural disasters; I'd shrink in the face of shameful breaches of justice and decency.

When your ears and mouth are stopped, when you have shrunk into tinyness, the horrors hardly impact on you; your faith in a loving God and in the basic goodness of humankind are not asked to respond to any challenge. Most times the ear-blocking and the mouth-stopping and the shrinking to the point of invisibility worked; but sometimes the trick failed to work and then it was my faith in a loving God and in the fundamental goodness of humankind that shrank instead.

But, unexpectedly, an epiphany happens: grace flows in a moment of showing forth, a moment of clarification and illumination, a moment not consciously sought but given as a blessing. I was gifted with such a moment as I attempted to shrink from the images showing the horrific aftermath of the Asian tsunami. Lines from Patrick Kavanagh flamed into my mind:

> Oh God, can a man find you when he lies with his face
> downwards
> And his nose in the rubble that was his achievement?
> Is the music playing behind the door of despair?

I noticed that in the garden a snowdrop had pushed against a frozen clod of earth to shine its small light. I knew then if I didn't know before that it is not by shrinking we keep our faith in a loving God; it is not by stopping our mouths and our ears that we experience the glory of the goodness of humankind. It is by opening ourselves to the suffering of others, sharing in it fully, listening to the pitiful cries of the grieving with open ears and echoing them with open mouths, weeping their tears with open eyes that we see the face of a loving God; that we know the cruelly dead have been gathered up to sweet rest; that we know it is out of the rubble of desolation the flower of human courage pushes its way upwards bearing with grace and care its beautiful consoling.

Anger

The other day I found myself weak with anger. I was sitting at the kitchen table reading the paper when I came upon a report which engulfed me gradually in waves of horror, revulsion and, finally, a huge, paralysing, speechless anger. The report had to do with the alleged abuse of children by their father. It described a reign of terror and violence which had lasted over a period of years during which the lives of the innocent, the trusting, the vulnerable had been wrenched and twisted into a shape so horribly pitiful that the account of it would have drawn tears of blood from a stone.

'Weak with anger' – it is a significant expression, isn't it? Anger, which weakens one, renders one powerless. Or is it the pointlessness in the face of horrors we seem to be unable to do anything about which weakens our anger?

I've always had trouble with anger; I've never known what to do with it. As a child I was taught that it was a deadly sin – and certainly angry outbursts, for whatever reason, were not tolerated by my mother in our house. She always claimed darkly that such displays of ire did not come from her side of the family; all belonging to her were gentle people for generations back, she would say, with a sidelong glance at my father. 'An eye for an eye, a tooth for a tooth' wrestled with 'blessed are the meek' and the gentle urge to 'turn the other cheek'.

So what does one do with anger? God knows there is enough happening around us to be angry about. The newspaper report which affected me so traumatically the other day can be matched in horror by numberless others: reports of man's inhumanity to man are not hard to find, reports that fill one with impotent rage. I have always suspected that anger expressed or unexpressed is destructive; that it is such a disturbingly frightening emotion it is bound to harm one in some way.

Though Christ became angry with the moneylenders, he remained strong, uncorrupted by his anger. Ah, but, I have just reminded myself, his anger did not preclude love: his anger was born out of love and led into love. I think I have got somewhere now. Anger doesn't need to weaken: it can strengthen if it is wedded to love. The anger we feel over the abused little ones we are unable to help can energise us into cherishing all the more the children who are in our lives, within our ambits.

Anger against injustice, against violence, against any form of inhumanity can energise us into becoming more human, more heartful, more just in our own lives. Anger if it is wedded to love, centred in love, can be a force for creative change for good. It's a thought, isn't it?

Listening again

There was a time, long, long ago, when my father was the handsomest, strongest, most intelligent man in the whole world; and my mother was the wisest woman. I don't remember when exactly my opinion of them began to change – but at any rate, by the time I was in my teens I was convinced that neither of them knew anything worth knowing. In fact, I used to look at them sometimes and marvel that someone like me could ever have sprung from such a dull pair. I used to feel a kind of contemptuous pity for their grey lives, relieved by little more than a mottled anxiety about living.

My own life, I was gratified to acknowledge, was awash with dazzling colour, full of exciting questions and speculations, dizzying awarenesses and insights. It was intoxicating to feel myself on the breathtaking edge of discovery – and vital to free myself from the deadening hand of my parents' rule.

Now my parents are old. My father may have lost most of his physical strength and mobility to arthritis, but his understanding is undimmed, his humour unbowed, his love for my mother undiminished. My mother's wisdom glows quietly, constantly.

'Let him go,' she said to me recently, referring to my son who is at college and whose lightheartedness about his future causes me to fret sometimes. 'Let him go. You've both given him your best – and it shows! Can't you see it?' And I was grateful to her for stilling my fears.

When I visit them, I love to be drawn into their small warm circle. I can't bear to contemplate a world without them. I listen intently to their every word and hoard them away carefully, safely. Their simple faith in God casts away doubt; their philosophical acceptance of old age and mortality move me unutterably. They are ready; I am not. I tried to say this to my father recently, to tell him I was sorry for having lived so much of my life without them, for having run out on them.

'You didn't run out on us,' he said with a chuckle. 'Didn't you see us opening the door!'

The culture of blame

We all do it: blame each other. We do it all the time. We teach our children to do it very early: I've experienced a three-year-old doing it with the accomplished ease of a seasoned practitioner. Teenagers do it with a great deal of belligerence and bluster; older people do it with an unattractive self-righteousness which signposts depressingly towards complacency. I do it myself with all the linguistic resources at my disposal to screen off the weaknesses in my case.

I had a thought the other day while I was in mid-rant about the current parlous state of the world. I had no trouble at all firing off salvos of blame: the intransigence of those politicians; the greed and hypocrisy of that country; the failure of organised religions to heal the world; the night-time barking of the neighbour's dog; the sheer stupidity and irresponsibility of men, in general, who should never be let near an open flame, let alone rule the world.

All at once I felt nauseated; sick of my own ranting, over-glutted on my own self-righteousness, which is both the prerequisite and the afterglow of blame-laying. I thought: what if I and everyone else in the world miraculously stopped laying blame and, as a way of shouldering some responsibility for this earth, just as Tolkien suggests, vowed to till our own patch to the best of our ability, leaving it in a better state than we had found it in and passing it on to our children freely and hopefully? Just think of the changes we could effect if we all stopped blaming one another, everyone from the least powerful to the most powerful, and simply took responsibility for making things better on our own sphere of influence, our own patch of earth. Blaming others releases us from vital obligations. The culture of blame that we are industriously fashioning today will deprive our children of the opportunity to grow tall and straight.

> If only there were evil people somewhere insidiously committing evil deeds, and it were necessary only to separate them from the rest of us to destroy them. But the line dividing good and evil cuts through the heart of every human being. And who is willing to destroy a piece of his own heart?
>
> ALEKSANDR SOLZHENITSYN

In a world where everyone blames everyone else, refusing to acknowledge the mote in our own eye, truth, self-discipline, responsibility for our actions and obligations towards others stagnate. We are stuck in the foul standing water, dreaming, perhaps, of clean-flowing streams, rivers and cascades, and wondering how we lost them – but, you can be sure, blaming one another for the loss.

Completing the circle

My parents separated this summer. After fifty years spent weaving together the uneven tapestry of marriage, my father tried, and failed, to whisper some words to my mother, sank low into his chair and covered his eyes as the ambulance men wheeled her out of the kitchen, down our long, narrow hall, through the front door, along the little garden, now showing sad signs of missing her hand, and into the waiting ambulance.

Hovering anxiously the night before, I had heard my mother speak from her bed across to my father. 'Will you miss me?' My father, normally quite deaf, miraculously heard her first time. 'And why wouldn't I miss you!' he answered. 'Will you miss me?' 'I will,' she said softly, and then more firmly, 'and I want this house and all its business conducted from now on as if I were still here. Do you hear me? I don't want anyone coming into this house in my absence that I wouldn't approve of.' I waited for my octogenarian, arthritic, temperate father to retaliate with a joke as would normally be his wont, but instead he said quite seriously, still remarkably undeaf, 'This house will be conducted from tomorrow on as if you are still sitting in your own chair opposite me. You can rest assured of that.' And my mother sighed with satisfaction. 'Ah sure, you know I trust you,' she whispered into the silence.

And now she was journeying to a small nursing home, her new home, the place where her failing health dictates she must spend the rest of her days. The location is where she was born and reared, and which she has always described as heaven on earth. We passed the sturdy farmhouse that had both limited and nurtured her young girl's dreams – but she was looking straight ahead and I trembled at what I thought might be fear in her eyes.

Were we doing the right thing? Her doctor had said she needed round-the-clock care, the kind of care she would only receive in a nursing home. It had seemed like a miracle when a place became available near her homestead, her own heaven on earth, where she would be able to see in the distance her father's fields, now husbanded by his grandson. But suddenly I wasn't sure any more. All my trust in my own judgement, my motives, deserted me. My mind raced here and there. Years before, I had asked my parents to come and live with me. Had I felt a trace of relief when they had both reacted in horror at the mere notion of leaving their own place? I couldn't be sure.

We arrived. Kind hands helped my mother inside. She was shown her room. 'That's nice,' she said, pointing to the blue satin coverlet on her bed. 'What do you think?' I asked her later, nervously. She looked at me steadily. 'It isn't what I want,' she said, 'I want to be in my own home with your father – but I know I have to be here. You know,' she continued, 'I'm back where I started. I've done a small circle. That seems right, somehow.' She took my hand, 'I have complete trust in your father and in God.'
'And in me,' I begged her silently through a blinding haze of tears. 'Tell me you trust me too.'

21

A couple of strokes
in the right direction

A friend said to me some years ago, while looking me
straight in the face, 'You don't trust easily, do you?' I was
taken aback by the unexpectedness of her words,
especially as I had just seen her through a rough patch in
her life. I thought all was openness and trust between us.
She continued, 'You have no problem reaching out to
people, offering sympathy, understanding – I mean,
you're a great friend. But you don't give anyone else an
opportunity to do the same for you.' I experienced a
sickening sensation that my cover had just been blown.
Head and gut effected a swift integration – and I knew in
that instant that she was right. I was horribly
embarrassed. I wanted to adopt a foetal position in a
corner and weep. It was true: I offered others what I
wanted for myself but I didn't trust them enough to ask
for it. I trusted God all right, but I didn't trust him in
other people. I had lulled myself into a false sense of ease,
seeing myself as open, sympathetically imaginative – the
kind of person you can trust not to sit in judgement but
to understand. A great cover for a basic lack of trust in
other people, wouldn't you agree?

I would like to say that this revelation acted as a decisive turning point in my life, but it didn't – a gentle curve, maybe! It's strange, significant, the way things come together – eventually even gentle curves create a circle. This summer, you see, a most extraordinary thing happened to me. At the ripe age of umpty um, I swam for the first time in my life. I had been terrified of being under water ever since I nearly drowned in an icy Galway river when I was six. A ten-year-old tearaway, known locally as Killer Canavan, had a particular aversion to small girls dithering on river-banks, so he pushed me in. Although I continued to enjoy the glorious life of the river, splashing and larking about to my heart's content, all subsequent efforts to swim ended in failure. One swallow of water would have me gasping, thrashing and flailing about in panic, my feet scrabbling for a hold on something solid. This summer I let go and I swam. I did. My husband told me just to call him Job: he promised that he would stay with me, dripping patience, until I made it. He suggested that I learn to float first and I agreed, provided that he kept hold of my chin – or any other bit of me, for that matter. I warned him not to leave me for a second, even if I appeared to be swimming like a fish. One sunny afternoon, floating on my back, I looked up into his kind, bearded face and said quietly, 'You can let go now. I'm going to be alright.' He let go. A familiar sensation of panic swept through me and I almost started my usual scrabble for a foothold. But I didn't. I just knew that if I trusted the water to keep me up, it would. And it did. It took my panic and laughed it away – and I laughed too as I free-floated effortlessly.

The following morning I slipped down to the sea on my own. 'Here goes,' I said to myself, plunged forward into

23

the water, executed three or four ungainly breaststrokes, swallowed a gallon or two of water – and didn't drown! Oh God, I felt so good. Trust! I was swimming in it – overflowing with it. Well, it's a couple of strokes in the right direction, isn't it?

Trust me

The son and heir, the one and only, the pride and joy, the source of my greatest happiness and deepest, nameless anxieties, had graduated from university. He wanted to be a writer. He wanted to write the definitive twentieth-century novel on Thursday after his takeaway. He also wanted to be a famous investigative journalist, immediately, if not sooner!

When he told me this, my heart quailed at thoughts of him starving alone in the Big City while hard, cynical editors, unmoved by his obvious talents, slammed door after door in his face. They would crush his spirit with their cold indifference, I thought, and then probably give the job to some lumpkin from pimpledom who can't even do joined-up writing but whose father is one of their biggest advertisers.

'Would you not think of doing a post-graduate course?' I urged him, knowing full well that it was myself I was thinking of. It would suit me fine to have him protected for another year from the world of work – or no work! 'No, Mum,' was his response. 'I want to start making my own way now – not next year. Trust me, Mum. I know I'm doing the right thing.'
'Trust me' his eyes had begged when he was seven and

wanted to go to the shop on his own. I let him go alright – then I sneaked to the corner of the lane to watch for him coming back, darting quietly out of sight as soon as I spotted his blue gansy come into view.

'Trust me' he had said when he was twelve and his Aunt and Uncle had offered to take him off to the States with them for a holiday. I let him go, put myself in debt with the dint of transatlantic phone calls, and didn't sleep a wink until we reclaimed him at the airport three weeks later.

'Trust me' he had said when he switched from Science to pure English at University. 'I know I'm doing the right thing.' And my days and nights were haunted with fears that he'd never settle.

And now 'Trust me' he was saying once more – and again my insides were dissolving in anxiety. 'What do you think?' I asked himself. 'Trust him,' he replied.

'What do you think?' I asked the Aunt and Uncle. 'Make him do a post-graduate course,' they said. 'It'll give him a better chance. The Big City is a hard place. He'll end up demoralised when he can't get a job.' 'Make him'! That couldn't be right. With a sigh, I settled myself to an eternity of worrying and planned an immediate food parcel.

He came home at the weekend. Yes, he'd had doors slammed in his face. No, he hadn't been able to find a permanent job. Yes, the food parcels were quare and welcome. But his faith in himself was undiminished, his optimism unchecked. And there was one editor in the Big City who had opened a door for him. With great glee he produced two articles he'd had published in a magazine and for which he was paid the princely sum of £80. He might just as well have been brandishing his first million. 'I told you I could do it, Mum,' he said, as he handed me a gansy to darn. 'Now aren't you glad you trust me to do things my way?' I suddenly felt as if every prayer I had ever said for him had been answered at once. 'I am, son,' I said, 'I am, indeed.' And a weight slipped noiselessly from my heart.

A sea change

Several years ago, shortly after my mother's death, a friend called to see me. This friend is a man of few words: an intensely private man.

'From now on, Mary,' he said quietly, 'you will find yourself having an entirely new relationship with your mother. Remember, she is now beyond misunderstanding.' Without fully understanding his words, my heart instinctively acquiesced to them. And rightly so. Over the following months my relationship with my mother underwent a profound change. And now it is indeed beyond misunderstanding, beyond doubt, beyond failure. Before it was sometimes troubled. I needed so much from her: unquestioning love and approval being the very least of my demands. When my brother died as a teenager, leaving me an only child, my mother's grief frightened me, struck terror into my heart's core. The substance is gone, I thought, and only the shadow is left. That was the image of myself that I carried about for years: a shadow, powerless to fill the empty space my brother had left. As a shadow I drifted about the edges of my parents' lives, hugging corners. I craved words – words of comfort and reassurance. I wanted to burrow my way in beyond my mother's grief and hear her tell me strongly that I had always held first place in her heart. It is only now that I can make such a painful admission. It is only now I know that the needy, tormented and tormenting girl I once was is understood and forgiven.

Now my communication with my mother is beyond words. In silence I understand everything. In silence my heart overflows with understanding. In silence her love flows over me and a great burden has lifted from me because now there is no need to tread warily the sometimes dangerous ground of words. Her death has given me the gift of being able, almost, to tap into eternity – into a vastness of peace, of understanding, of rest; a world of silence pregnant with love.

I know that the gift has implications for me here and now among the living. If I know, as I do know, that there is a world beyond words, beyond misunderstanding, beyond the thorny undergrowth of personal need; if I know that the heart can communicate powerfully and truthfully in silence, know the essence of another on a bright road which has no twists or turns, no hidden dark places, then I must surely know that the gifts of eternity are possible for me, here and now, among the living!

I wonder if I will be able to stay on the bright road; I wonder if I will be able to overcome a tendency to take refuge in a dark place, down a side-road, my heart heavy with hurt and resentment, my eyes blind with self-pity, my steps laboured under a weight of misunderstanding! Time will tell.

When it's not so easy to love

I was driving through the Donegal hills recently on my way back from a visit to the west of Ireland, when I suddenly realised I had forgiven someone who had hurt me a long time before. I didn't know how or when it had happened; I was only aware that it had: that I no longer harboured the bitterness I had long learned to associate with this person's name. In its place was a sympathetic understanding I couldn't remember having arrived at. I rounded a familiar bend on the road and glanced automatically to my left where the expanse of lake water lay glittering in the spring sunshine. I felt light, unburdened; the air, even in the car, was mountain fresh and clean. I felt as if I was the one who had been forgiven, and then I remembered someone's words, C.S. Lewis's, I think, that forgiving and being forgiven are two names for the same thing.

The person I had forgiven was someone about whom I had cared for deeply. As I continued my journey I found myself reflecting on how much easier it is to forgive those we love; how easy it is to stay loving those who are dear to us; how easy it is to persuade ourselves that our lives are filled with love, that we operate out of the Christian Doctrine of Love, because there are those in our lives we have no trouble loving, no trouble forgiving, no trouble at all.

What about those who are hard to love, hard to forgive: those who frighten us, disgust us or appal us; those who fill us with loathing; those we perceive as bullies, manipulators, liars and hypocrites? They are not so easy to love or forgive and yet this is precisely the challenge which faces us every day: our Christian Faith challenges us to love our enemies. That's not easy, is it?

When I got back home there was a letter waiting for me from a friend in America; it contained an excerpt from Rabbi Michael Lenner's *How Can I Find God?*

> Raise children. Teach them that there is power in the universe that makes for the possibility of healing and transformation, and that that power is what others mean when they talk about God. Always be aware of the ways in which that which is, is in the process of becoming that which ought to be and make yourself part of the process.

I had my answer.

The wedding

The day before, the hills were lost in veils of mist; the sun's efforts to warm the city were thwarted persistently by bad-tempered, iron-clad clouds. It did not bode well for the following day – and I had promised them glorious sunshine. The sun will shine, I had insisted; our prayers will be answered; the weather forecasters don't know what they are talking about. And they had both looked at me gratefully, willing me, trusting me to be right.

Well, the following morning I experienced the inexpressible pleasure of having been part of a miracle. The sun was firmly in control; the clouds had been banished elsewhere; the air was sweet, fresh, new-washed and I offered fervent prayers of thanksgiving to a God, who, I felt suddenly with a warm burst of happiness, was personal and loving by my side.

When we arrived at the church our son was there before us – tall, elegant in his wedding finery. I was struck by what I can only call his otherness in a way I had experienced once before: when they had placed him in my arms seconds after his birth. A huge, panic-edged feeling of loss lodged in my throat and threatened to choke me. Unbidden, a hundred claims on his life rushed to the surface of my mind, only to fall about me in confusion and bewilderment. This near-stranger was well and truly master of his own ship now.

As they spoke their vows in their clear, young voices I wondered if every other person in the congregation felt the same overwhelming sense of the beauty and truth of the words as I did, and I wondered if they felt, as I did, why the memory of those strong beautiful vows fails so often to overcome selfish need and stubborn pride.

I'd been invited to read the Epistle:

> Love is always patient and kind; love is never boastful or conceited; it is never rude or selfish; it does not take offence, and is not resentful.
>
> 1 CORINTHIANS 13:4-6

Love has revealed to me so clearly the quiet way towards peace of mind, heart and soul, and yet I so often choose the noisy marketplace, bargaining and squabbling over prices with the best of them. But I hold the island safely within, obscured at times, I know, behind mists of painful confusion, yet always willing to show itself, sunlit and still, if I take the time to stand and see with those other eyes, my clear eyes, the eyes that never dim and wear out – because they are the eyes that have seen the glory of the Lord.

I murmured a prayer for reassurance that I had done my best as a mother and that my best had not dimmed the glory of the otherness they had placed in my arms all those years ago.

No waiting! It's instant!

They say you're old when memories of your youth take up permanent residence in your head and jostle for place with the present. I must be in rehearsal mode because, in a version of the above, more and more I find myself going back in time to recover memories but not, may I add, to compete with the present; rather to try to make sense of it. Here's one.

We were seventeen. Our friend, Joan, had learned to drive and we were now huddled in her parents' hallway, a frantic, nail-biting little group, waiting for her father to pronounce on our future – well, on the summer ahead, at least. Would he give the family jalopy to Joan to take us to a dance twenty miles away? Because if he did, the likelihood of his doing it again was on the cards, thus ensuring that our seventeenth summer was going to be heaven on earth – if we didn't all die of an unbearable happiness first. Joan came out to us, an ecstatic grin splitting her face in two. Her father followed her, casually, catching us in the middle of miming fervent thank you's heaven-ward. He handed Joan a sheet of paper. 'By the way,' he said, these are the responsibilities that go with driving the car.' There were five – and they calmed us down significantly.

Joan reneged on one of them a month later and we were without the jalopy for the month of July. We had all shared in the joy; now we all shared the blame. It made sense. Rights, freedoms, had responsibilities attached. We genuinely accepted that as a profound, unalterable truth, regardless of how often we offended against it or tried to get round it. It went along with our unfamiliarity with the concept of 'instant gratification'.

We were reared to wait. 'You can't put on Radio Luxembourg until your father has finished listening to "Hundred Best Tunes".' 'I'm sorry, but I'll just have to let down last year's dresses for you; you'll have to wait until next year for new ones.' Waiting was second nature to us and we invested what was being waited for with enormous importance, as well as an acknowledgement of the responsibilities that went with its eventual acquisition.

And now! Well, there's instant food; instant music; instant entertainment; instant pleasure. We want it all and we want it now. No waiting. No responsibilities. Instant gratification. Instant solutions.

I think we should learn to wait again. I really believe it makes what is being waited for more worthwhile!

A dream of summer

I walked by the river one evening recently and the
heartaching sweetness of spring was in the air. The
disembodied voices of children floated back to me from
further down the lough shore; a high piping medley of
shouts, pleas, laughter; and for a few moments I was
involuntarily catapulted back into the past. One of the
children's voices became my own, the others' those of my
childhood friends as we responded, in the way that children
instinctively do, to the warming of the airs, to the
whispered promise of an eternal summer.

The long incarceration in the darkness of winter was over.
St Patrick's Day had been and gone and, as always, the
world was different afterwards; things were happening
underground that you could hear if you listened hard
enough: movings, shiftings, little sighs, breathings: the first
daffodil; the first crocus; the first primrose. Birdsong
became lusty and we all joined in.

We wanted to play outside again. 'Calling' for each other
was back: 'Hello, Mrs O'Neill. I'm here to call for Julie. Is
she coming out to play?' Winter pallor gave way to rosy
faces. We would invariably head for the river, the part of it
that meandered through a small wood, and there, in 'our'

clearing, we would remind the river with skimmers, flat stones that we would send flying over its surface, that it was time to get ready for summer.

This part of the river and this clearing would, later on in summer, resound to our mighty yells and splashes as we braved the water, which remained ice-cold even on the hottest day. The heart-stopping cold was part of the fun. We tested our courage on it. Who would jump in first without being pushed from behind? But, for now, when summer was only a promise, we communicated with the river through our skimmers. Get ready! Get ready, our skimmers would sing to the river. We'll be back soon. All that spice and all that joy responding to the miraculous movement of spring. The wood seemed a safe place then; a place that seemed to be in sympathy with our springtime dream of a perfect summer.

Back in the present, I had caught up with the children whose voices I'd heard earlier. They were skimming stones along the surface of the water, their voices still piping out a medley of laughter and high spirits. Their rosy faces seemed achingly familiar.

A springtime dream of a perfect summer. Safety, I thought as I passed them. Safety would be good. May their summer be safe at least.

Polarities

What but a soul could have the wit
To build me up for sin so fit.
FROM 'A DIALOGUE BETWEEN THE SOUL AND BODY'
BY ANDREW MARVELL

A couple of lines from a seventeenth-century poem that came into my mind the other day. You know the way things sometimes slip into your mind, apparently unsolicited, and quietly offer themselves up as the theme of a bout of contemplation? It is only later that you begin to make connections between what seemed at the time to be random rags and scraps thrown up by your memory – bits of poems, other readings, odd encounters – and you realise that your soul was working towards some kind of epiphany, some kind of revelation, all the time.

This poem is in the form of a dispute between the flesh and the spirit conducted along the lines of a domestic ding-dong. It turns into quite a nasty little tussle, each party blaming the other for all the ills of its existence. 'You keep me imprisoned within your bony shackles,' the soul protests shrilly – in so many words – 'and your flesh weighs me down, smothers me'.

'And you,' responds the body – again, I hasten to add, in so many words – 'are a party-pooper who tries to deny me the slightest bit of pleasure. You won't be happy until I'm dead!'

And so on. Any attempt at drawing together, any attempt at mutuality, at a more enriched existence through fusion, doesn't get a look in. It is mutual exclusivity all the way.

Nothing much changes, does it! Polarities, either/ors: bodies or souls; hearts or minds; reason or intuition; male or female; light or dark. To commit to one is to deny the other. We were brought up to recognise opposites and keep them in their places: as far apart as possible. Walk in the light by closing your eyes to the dark. Close your mind to it. Listen to your head; your heart will lead you astray. Bad people are a breed apart; they have nothing to do with you. And so on.

We yearn for oneness with God and yet we are afraid to look at the polarities within ourselves, let alone try to unite them; we haven't the courage to draw the opposites together, unite them on the ground of love, make them one. Surely in any dialogue between the heart and the mind the happy resolution has to be the fusion of the polar opposites: the drawing together of the knowledge, the experience, the unmet needs which incite judgement and rejection, and the unconditional love which is an end in itself, which is beyond all judgement, all refusal. I think I read that somewhere!

There is a religious fable in a book called *The Healing Power of Illness*: an ascetic who was meditating in a cave was annoyed by a mouse who scurried in and began nibbling at his sandal. 'I'm hungry,' the mouse squeaked in response to the ascetic's irate challenge to its disturbing activity. 'Go away, silly mouse,' said the ascetic. 'I am seeking oneness with God. How could you think of disturbing me?' 'How do you propose to become one with God,' asked the mouse, 'if you can't even become one with me?'

The island

That summer, himself and myself spent a week on the smallest and, to my mind, the loveliest of the islands off the west coast. We flew over in a little plane which indecently laid bare to my shocked eyes, not only its mechanical innards, but also its pilot. My customary consolation when flying – that God aided by a formidably-focused me is the power keeping the thing up – was thus cruelly exploded. I had my eyes shut tightly during the landing, fortunately missing what himself described graphically to me afterwards: the sight of a small boy shooing a string of donkeys off the grassy patch which served as a runway, and then giving a delighted thumbs-up sign to the pilot who, by this time, was describing his third circle of the island.

During that week the island was a magical place, its grey slate stretches warmed by the sun. The clean Atlantic air unblocked every corner of my mind leaving me free and open as a child, so that I marvelled constantly at everything: the peace and profound silence held by the little walled fields; the deep pine-water wells; the strangely exotic plants and flowers blossoming among the flat limestone rocks.

On the highest point of the island there was a small graveyard looking out to sea, and from the moment I spied it from the rocks below, I felt compelled to visit it. I climbed up there on our third morning and immediately was disappointed to find someone there already. He was sitting on a gravestone chewing a blade of grass, looking out over the sea. He glanced round at me briefly and nodded, unsmiling: a weird-looking figure, slight, about sixteen, with a city-pale face and long reddish hair. He was wearing what looked like his father's coat: a huge black affair. I wished he'd go. I wandered among the gravestones telling over the names of the men, women and children who'd lived and died on the island. Their quiet presences reached out to me and touched me in such a friendly human way that I could feel tears start up behind my eyes. I'd forgotten about the weird red-haired youth until his voice startled me.

'Isn't it only brilliant here,' he was saying in a pronounced Dublin accent. 'You can feel it too, can't you?'
I nodded. We shared a gravestone and sat looking out to sea. He told me he visited his grandparents on the island every year.
'I spend most of my time up here,' he said. 'I love it up here. Everything I don't understand sort of comes right up here. D'ye know what I mean?'
'I think I do,' I said. We sat in silence.
'Isn't it funny the way the dead can seem more alive than the living!' he said, as we climbed through the stile leading to the road.
'James Joyce thought the same,' I said.
'Who?' he asked. 'Oh, him! Bloomsday and all that!'

We waved goodbye to each other.

The darkling thrush

I leant upon a coppice gate
When frost was spectre-grey
And winter's dregs made desolate
The weakening eye of day.

FROM 'THE DARKLING THRUSH' BY THOMAS HARDY

More than a hundred years ago, Thomas Hardy, the great
English poet and novelist, penned a moving lyric called
'The Darkling Thrush'. It is the end of the day, the end of
the year, the end, in fact, of the century. Nature has
contracted: 'the ancient pulse of germ and birth/ Is
shrunken hard and dry'; the grey landscape is ghost-
haunted; the poet, along with every other creature on
earth, is fervourless, out of tune, hopeless.

Suddenly, the gloom is exploded by the thrilling, full-
hearted song of a thrush. This is no brash, impatient young
bird cocking a snook at misery, striking a defiant attitude in
the face of an uninspiring, spiritless old world; this is 'an
aged thrush, frail, gaunt and small / with blast-beruffled
plume' who has launched his song of joy and hope. This is a
weather-beaten, life-battered old bird who is singing of
hope. And the poet is wonder-struck. He looks about him.
Where has the thrush found cause for singing? He

concludes that although he can see no cause for hope, the thrush knows better:

> So little cause for carroling
> Of such ecstatic sound
> Was written on terrestrial things
> Afar or nigh around,
> That I could think there trembled through
> His happy, good-night air
> Some blessed hope whereof he knew
> And I was unaware.

I love this poem. It is ironic that old gloom-and-doom Hardy should be the one who makes the definitive statement for me about human hope – its independence of circumstances; its incorruptibility; its unexpectedness; its courage and beauty; its stubborn tenacity – its thrilling full-throated song forever challenging the gloom. As someone spreads darkness, someone else lights a candle. As women and children weep, love shows his face unexpectedly. In the midst of atrocity, a healing hand reaches out to offer comfort. In a trough of lies, truth reveals its shining face.

Long may the song of the aged thrush resound with full-throated ease. Long may its song spring with thrilling unexpectedness in the human heart.

Forgiveness

My husband, with a sly glance at my face, flushed and cross because he'd forgotten to collect the dry cleaning on his way home from work, said with high good humour and a sanctimonious expression: 'To err is human; to forgive is divine.' And off he went, whistling tunelessly, to air the dog. The incident was a typical piece of domestic trivia, but the words stayed in my head: 'To err is human; to forgive is divine.'

And then something else happened. I was producing the school musical and opening night was only days away. Right through rehearsals I'd been full of enthusiasm and heartfelt praise for the degree of commitment, talent, cooperation and generosity displayed by the cast and everyone else involved with the production. But now the nerves were in shreds; and I'd pulled a muscle in my back, because I just can't resist joining in actively with everything going on on stage – forgetting that my dancing days are over.

I roared at a youngster for missing a cue. In fact, she hadn't missed it at all – I was the one who had lost her place! The child's shocked face and panic-stricken eyes cut me like a knife as I realised my mistake. When I apologised to her later and asked her to forgive me for having bawled her out in the wrong, she said simply through her tears: 'It's all right, Miss; I know you're under pressure!' I could have wept at the beauty of her generosity and understanding.

So you see, the concept of forgiveness was on my mind. To know oneself is dependent on being known, understood by another, and forgiveness is somewhere at the heart of the process. To be forgiven is beautiful. To err is human; to forgive is divine. When we forgive or are forgiven we are touched by the divine, we are in harmony with the divine. We believe in a God who knows us, understands us, accepts us, forgives us when we trespass against him. But human nature does not forgive easily. Unforgiveness is often bred into our minds, our hearts, into the marrow of our bones.

And yet to experience the divine in someone's forgiveness for us, in our forgiveness for another, is to experience a power and beauty that frees our hearts and minds from the darkness of fear.

Rianna

My father died in the winter of his days on a dark day in November; my granddaughter was born on the wing of a dawn in December, the brightest dawn of the year, a dawn which sang of life and love and hope, of a dream fulfilled. Her birth moved me with gentle joy from mourning into morning.

My father's generous spirit was close to me. I had sat beside him, holding his hand, watching as his face gradually assumed the awesome, remote dignity of one who is passing fearlessly from one state of being to another, of one to whom the great mystery has already been partly revealed. And now his great granddaughter was with us, calling us to life. I remembered words from the poet Kahlil Gibran and they shone with a new radiance:

> You would know the secret of death. But how shall you find it unless you seek it in the heart of Life?
> The owl whose night-bound eyes are blind until the day cannot unveil the mystery of light.
> If you would indeed behold the spirit of death, open your heart wide unto the body of life.
> For life and death are one, even as the river and the sea are one.
>
> THE PROPHET

We had to wait four days before we could travel to see our grandchild – this living proof that God was in his heaven and all was right with the world; this child in whose face I was hoping to see the loved ones I had lost, who was going to recover for me the wonders I had misplaced, the hope that had dimmed with the years, the unfulfilled dreams.

When finally I looked into her perfect face what overwhelmed me was a heartbreaking sweet sense of her otherness – her uniqueness; the same sense of an infant's otherness I had felt all those years before when I had first held her father in my arms. I knew I could never, would never, burden her with my needs; I knew that she was a joy to be watched as she flew, not one to be grasped and held.

I wrote my beautiful granddaughter a poem:

Rianna
'A girl! She's perfect.' Your father's
Voice came bearing down the line
Your weight of wonder cradled in the
Circle of your mother's long, bright night.
And all that day, a hundred miles from
Where your shining, new perfection lay,
My arms would come together of their own
Accord, and hold the lightness of your being close.

Already on your unknown face I'd set
My brother's eyes, my father's smile, my mother's
High cheekbones. I ached to recognise in you
The daughter lost before she came to birth.
And then, when you were four days old
I knelt beside your crib and wept within

To see your perfect face, so much your own,
Wear one small frown to have to bear the
Weight of someone else's loss and hopes.
I drew aside from you the blanket of my need,
And in the wonder of your otherness
I breathed, 'You're New!'

Being wrong

It can be chastening to experience as a result of the blast of a new insight, a hitherto devoutly held conviction rocking on its foundations. Frightening, even. Certainly disturbing. In a world that is changing daily before our very eyes, and often it seems unpleasantly so, it is comforting to have certainties to hold onto – to know with solid assurance that this is such or that is so.

It feels good to be right about certain things. We often quote one indisputable truth to support another in the making: 'As sure as night follows day', we say or, 'as sure as I woke up this morning'. There is something deeply satisfying about being in the comfort zone where one and one make two; where winter moves into spring; where we know the right answer to a question.

Nobody likes to be wrong. Being wrong has unhappy connotations of the childhood classroom: getting your sums wrong; feeling stupid; feeling inadequate; feeling the misery of standing outside the magic circle made by those who always have the right answers.

I hate being wrong. I've been known to call in the services of countless experts in support of a point of view that I'm pushing in an argument or discussion. Himself stopped believing in the existence of these experts years ago, so I confess now that yes, I used to make most of them up as I went along, in my zeal to be right.

However, despite my addiction to the comfort zone of being right, I do know that to discover and to acknowledge one has been wrong, that one's thesis is fundamentally flawed, can be one of the most liberating of human experiences. To open oneself to another point of view can result in a journey to a place breathtaking in its newness, dizzying in the challenges it offers.

For the ardent feminist who allows herself to empathise for even a moment with some of the pain and confusion of the male; for the male who looks directly at the shameful injustices perpetrated against women; for black and white, old and young, rich and poor, friend and foe, to be able to crawl inside each other's skins sometimes, to be able to leave the narrow comfort zone of being right at all costs, is to take one's rightful place at life's feast – to share in the good things with others for whom there is also everything right with being wrong sometimes.

Passing on

My son and I were at a gathering recently when another guest remarked on what she saw to be a striking resemblance between us. The lad and I looked at each other and smiled – we're used to it. We can even see it ourselves in photographs. Although his height and colouring are his father's, the planes of his face, the set of his eyes he has undoubtedly inherited from me. And what's more, his little daughter, the world's most fascinating child incidentally, is now sporting the same stubborn cheekbones and chin. Her parents, somewhat darkly, I might add, also attribute to me her bright and bushy-tailed loquaciousness in the small hours of the morning.

People used to say, long ago, that I was the spitting image of my father. 'She has her mother's cheekbones right enough, but she's your double for all that, Michael,' they'd say, and my father would cock his head to one side and look at me appraisingly.

It is quite extraordinary to see a way of smiling, a pair of eyes, the set of a chin, the curve of a cheek, even a tone of voice, repeated down through the generations. It offers a kind of earthly immortality that is irresistible and a comforting sense of who we are.

No wonder then that people look so searchingly into the faces of infants to find a father's nose, a grandmother's smile, a mother's eyes. And in a wish to please, to flatter, to reassure, resemblances will be noted and flourished gladly whether they exist or not. I was once told I was 'scraped down' off a total stranger by someone who thought we were father and daughter – we were only standing at the same ice-cream counter!

And so great-grandfather's nose is passed down to our children for them to pass down to their children, modified, we hope, by great-grandmother's smile. And what else besides eyes and cheekbones is passed down which keeps the past alive? Not Uncle Willie's commitment to the bottle, we hope, nor Aunt Sarah's dangerous temper; and not, please God, the miserable streak of meanness running through Uncle Willie's family.

What about fear? Distrust? Failure of imagination? Hatred? Bigotry? Prejudice? What did we think when we saw earlier this year on television a group of young people discussing the future of Northern Ireland? The mouths that were tight with a familiar bitterness; the accusations and counter accusations; the weirdly familiar choking rage, failure to listen: where did it all come from, I'm sure we wondered. Where were they getting it from? Not from our side, anyway, we probably thought. From the other side doubtlessly. It has to be from the other side.

Friends

For a while there recently, I wasn't myself at all. My usual comedy scripts lay deep-buried under a weight of something dark and sad. I had lost my sense of humour somewhere and with it my sense of perspective, zest for life, faith, hope – all lost, and in their place an ill-defined sense of terror.

Television was a nightmare hurling horrors at me by the second: murder, violence, greed, despair – and turning it off didn't help at all; the terrors were still out there: I could feel them, smell them. 'The centre cannot hold' was written everywhere I looked: in the sky, on the ground, on walls and houses. The world seemed mindless. We were lemmings rushing towards the cliff edge and nobody, nobody was calling, Stop! Had God turned away his face?

And then a young girl turned the light on for me again – one of my students who caught up with me as I was walking out of school. She was obviously coming from an Art class because she was wearing a bright yellow badge of paint on her forehead. 'Do you smell it, Miss?' she asked, sniffing ecstatically. 'Do you smell the gorgeous evening? Isn't it only fantastic! Oh, dear God, it's great to be alive!' And she did a little 'burl', swinging her heavy satchel high in the air as though it had wings. 'Bye, Miss, see you tomorrow.' And she leaped onto the bus.

The air felt sweet and fresh on my skin. Brave new world indeed that had such creatures as my young friend in it. Later that evening, as I was peeling the spuds, I found myself reflecting with gratitude on the patterns of grace that have occurred in my life up to now: the spoken words that have suddenly glowed with meaning; words I have read that have reached out and stirred my soul with revelations. And my friend, whose wisdom has so often moved me forward when I was stuck fast; who has reminded me when I have forgotten that love is the answer and good will triumph.

My women friends. I called them tenderly to mind: the friends who came when I sat frozen, unable to cry, after miscarrying a long-awaited child; who filled my lap with tiny, fragile snowdrops and held me while the blessed tears came. The friend I've known since childhood; married to an alcoholic, still beautiful, still erect, still smiling. The friend who is so wise, so perceptive, so uncannily knowing that I think she would probably have been burned as a witch in an earlier time. The friend who often chooses to hide a tender and sensitive heart behind the most wicked wit I have ever experienced. Strong, tender, wickedly funny, marvellous women I am glad to number among my friends. Long may they live and prosper. Long may they laugh and love. May the rain always fall gently on their fields – not forgetting a young girl with a bright badge of hope on her forehead.

Tim

I feel disorganised, distressed, anxious and overworked. I suspect I might be inefficient. But thanks be to God, my colleagues appear to feel the same about themselves. Nevertheless, I find myself thinking more and more recently about my old friend, Tim, who has long gone to his rest.

I am a child again summer-holidaying at my grandfather's, running up the *boithrin* to Tim's thatched cottage, the smell of wild woodbine from the bramble bushes sending me wild with joy.

'Tim, Tim,' I scream, 'Your cows are all out on the road and there's one of them in Flaherty's yard scattering the hens.'
'Arrah, what matter,' Tim drawls, pulling slowly on his pipe, 'when they get tired moochin', they'll come home. Thanks be to God, isn't it a great day!'

Tim it was who introduced me to the best mushroom fields, which we plundered together in the early dew-fresh mornings – afterwards toasting them on turf embers to eat with our fingers. Tim knew where the wild strawberries and cherries grew and where to find the best

56

crab-apples for jelly. A fox couldn't dig a new den that Tim didn't know about within hours and he was on intimate terms with every badger's lair for miles around. He shared all these wonders with me and one day he taught me how to listen to the silence of the countryside around the lake, which wasn't silence at all of course but a slow, strange music of little breathings and chirpings and lapping.

'You've a big hole in the sleeve of your gansy, Tim,' I'd say severely.

'Arrah, no matter,' would be his response, issued lazily through clouds of pipe-smoke. 'Thanks be to God, I'm not in the running for a morning-suit.'

'You were robbed at the fair again, Tim,' my grandfather would growl. 'What kind of an *amadan* are you that you let your beasts go for next to nothing?'

'Arrah, no matter,' from Tim, as he leaned against the apple-garden wall and watched the progress of a cabbage butterfly. 'Thanks be to God, I have plenty and enough for my needs.'

'Well, you'll never die of ulcers anyway; that's one sure thing,' my grandfather would laugh, clapping Tim on the shoulder.

Remembering Tim, I tell myself to slow down and watch the cabbage butterfly instead of courting an ulcer. I know that Tim's world will never be wholly mine. My binding ties and commitments have already been woven. Perhaps the world is too much with me. I know I do not take enough time to stand and stare – and there are so many wonders, so much music, so many wild strawberries, so many dew-fresh mornings, all hidden behind a heavy veil of anxiety, fever and fret.

Tomorrow, I'm going to be still. Tomorrow I'm going to say, 'Arrah, what matter; thanks be to God, isn't it great to be alive.'

A world of equivocation

My mother made no distinction whatever between a downright lie and the slightest whiff of equivocation: with her, it was either the truth and nothing but the truth or a lie.

Like most children, there were times when I had an irresistible compulsion to alter the truth whenever I found the truth a bit on the dull side. Well, my imagination would be singing with sound and colour, bursting with richly fantastic characters of extraordinary eccentricity – and rarely could I resist plunging the bare truth into this bright, brimming well, until out it would come, gloriously embroidered, improved no end in my opinion.

'Great imagination that child has,' my father would marvel. 'She doesn't know the truth from a stone on the wall,' my mother would retort darkly and I would lie awake worrying at night. At school we learned by rote from the catechism that 'No lie can be lawful or innocent. No motive, however good, can excuse a lie, because a lie is always sinful and bad in itself'. But then, I knew people who wielded the truth like a blunt instrument. My cousin Kay, for instance, was partial to clubbing me senseless with the truth.

After a period of serious deliberation I decided I should always tell the truth if I was asked, I should confine my imagination to obvious works of fiction and I should never, ever tell anyone they looked like a sack of potatoes tied in the middle. Life became simple again and I slept the sleep of the just at night.

But now! Well, I never knew so many lies existed! I never knew they had so many shapes, so many twists and turns, so many disguises. Lies abound. They are everywhere and I cannot sort them out at all. The ones hardest of all to detect are, of course, the ones that masquerade as the truth. The whole world seems to be enmeshed betimes in a web of lies.

One person's truth is another person's lie. Men lie to women; women lie to men; both lie to themselves. Some will die rather than have the truth uncovered; others go mad. Relationships flounder in a tangle of lies. Truth lies buried under a heaving mass of equivocation. The other day I heard a person on the radio defending pornography on the grounds that it is impossible to prove that a diet of pornography has any adverse effect on those who consume it. What a mess of equivocation is there!

When did the truth become so hard to bear? So hard to find? So hard to hold onto? In times to come, when the chronicles of our age are being examined, maybe one claim to noteworthiness will turn out to be the blinding mastery with which we wielded the lie.

The adult world

The adult world, the world of experience, is greedy for the child, is charged with the need to take the mind of the child and cram it with facts, figures, attitudes, viewpoints, visions, perspectives. Isn't it true that often we insist that our children must be prepared to take, not their places in the world, but our places! Their minds must be attuned to ours. Our prejudices, our fears, our blind spots, our lies must be theirs also. Isn't it true that often we offer them a world soured with our own experience; to please us is their reason for being and on pain of losing our love they must follow in our footsteps, however leaden, sullen or dull those footsteps may be. But this is in contrast to the words of Jesus.

The disciples came to Jesus, saying, 'Who is the greatest in the kingdom of heaven?' And calling to him a child, he put him in the midst of them and said, 'Truly, I say to you, unless you turn and become like children, you will never enter the kingdom of heaven. Whoever humbles himself like this child, he is the greatest in the kingdom of heaven. Whoever receives one such child in my name receives me, but whoever causes one of these little ones who believe in me to sin, it would be better for him to have a great millstone fastened round his neck and to be drowned in the depth of the sea' (Matthew 8:1-5).

If we are not to usefully deafen our ears to Christ's words we must turn our faces, our minds and imaginations towards the innocent child and search there for wisdom, for truth. A child teaches us to accept unquestioningly the wonders of creation. A child knows the miracles to be found in a meadow. Who will teach him that God's created world is cracking under the sullen weight of man's greed? Who will teach him that his inheritance is being squandered, that his green fields are being turned to ash before he can rest his hot cheeks on their coolness, inhale their sweetness?

'Love one another as I have loved you,' Christ said. A child teaches us to love unconditionally. A child wakes, smiles and opens his arms wide to greet the sun and all those who live under it. A child teaches us that there are no separate compartments, no dividing walls, only infinite variety: a world 'incorrigibly plural'. Who will teach the child to love conditionally? Who will teach the child that Christ's words ought to be taken with a pinch of salt; that love is alright provided those we love are of the right creed and colour, think the right thoughts, sing the right songs, dance the right dances – 'right', of course, being that which is defined as 'right' by the teacher! And who is the teacher? The teacher is the adult who has lost forever the child of love and wonder who once dwelt within him.

> Unless you become like these, my little ones, you shall not enter into the kingdom of God.
>
> MATTHEW 18:3

A child teaches us to trust. Who will teach him suspicion? A child teaches us openness and directness. Who will teach him intrigue and subterfuge? A child teaches us to forgive with ease and grace. Who will teach him to harden his heart? A child teaches us to believe in miracles. Who will teach him cynicism?

And yet there is a world of love and trust and forgiveness just beyond the reaches of our hearts. There are miracles happening just on the edge of our understanding. There is a world beyond greed and hatred, a world of tenderness and generosity, fellowship and humanity, which is sung to us in a song, which we hear faintly between our sleeping and our waking.

Daniel

Daniel: a good name. A strong name with a fine biblical resonance to it. Daniel: the wise judge; Daniel: saved by God's intervention from the ferocious lions in the den. 'And on the seventh day the King came to lament over Daniel; on reaching the pit he looked inside, and there was Daniel, quite unperturbed' (Book of Daniel).

'Quite unperturbed'! I love that. In the midst of that murderous intent, the serene imperturbability of Daniel, the still centre. He had seen, after all, the face of God, known his intervention.

Seventeen years ago, here in Derry, Northern Ireland, a Daniel was born to Mary and John; and he grew daily in beauty and grace of mind and soul. A cruel dystrophic disease held his body in thrall, inhibiting his physical growth; but his mind and spirit ranged fearlessly over the vast spaces, regularly investigating the pockets of God for interesting surprises, testing, tasting the worlds of thought, of feeling, of ideas.

Within minutes of being in his company, one was captivated by the luminous beauty of his gaze and the sharp quizzical intelligence of his discourse. Once he played the piano for me: Chopin, I think it was. What I will never forget is the place to which he led my spirit that evening. For Daniel to play the piano meant several whole minutes devoted painstakingly to settling himself in front of the instrument and then several more getting his hands in position to play.

For the first minute or two, I found this agonising to watch and then my soul began to respond to the beauty of his exquisite patience, to the eminence of the mountain he was climbing; and I wept within in gratitude for the splendour of the view he showed me from the top. For days afterwards I walked in spirit with Daniel; serene, exquisitely patient, wisely centred.

For a brief moment, a moment which shone a bright light into the human heart, illuminating the places in which the best of us resides, for a moment which lasted a mere seventeen years, we had a Daniel in our midst. Daniel, born to Mary and John, raised within the strong circle of their love, frail of body but stronger than a lion in mind and spirit; Daniel, who passed on, calmly unperturbed, in his parents' arms this summer. Unperturbed: he had, after all, seen the face of God and known his intervention.

Paralysed by fear

I remember the first time I tasted fear: I was about three years old. I was sitting on top of our garden gate, swinging my legs and singing to myself; so thoroughly wrapped up in my own magical thoughts that I hadn't noticed the old woman's approach. She was lunging at me before I knew it, a black-clad, gnarled, witchy figure, bony fingers outstretched to grab me from my mother forever.

I screamed and fell backwards into the garden; the rest is a scrambled memory of hysterical, terrified sobbing, my arms tightly around my mother's neck, clutching for dear life, and the old woman (harmless, she turned out to be) apologising profusely for, inadvertently, having frightened me; it seems she had only stopped to admire me. I remember she tried to press a compensatory penny into my hand, but I wouldn't accept it, wouldn't look at her, kept my tearstained face pressed into my mother's neck.

The black-clad old woman, intentionally or not, had riven my golden world with the slash of fear and its concomitant of distrust. I would never again sit on top of our garden gate, swinging my legs and singing my song in the same state of perfect happiness.

Fear as an adaptive survival mechanism of childhood is one thing; fear in adult life can freeze the blood, cripple the mind and put iron limitations on the heart and soul. Fear is indeed a most potent agent of paralysis. Those who want to control others often use fear as the imprisoning chains. Think of the bully, the tyrant, the religious despot – fear is their weapon. As creatures made vulnerable by our knowledge of mortality, we are naturally prey to countless fears, which, if we were to allow them dominance over us, would contract our lives into a sunless, joyless struggle for survival.

The opposite of love is fear. It is love, and only love, that looks fear in the eye, challenges it and overcomes it. It is only love that recognises our reluctance to change, to transform, to let go, for what it is: fear. It is only love that sees beyond the shackles of fear to a place of true freedom, perfect light.

It is often the bright light of our own soul we are most afraid of, because if we were to live fully in that light, it would destroy our ego, free us into love; and so we foster fear as a defence against the light.

In a world where terror is used as a weapon to cripple others in mind, body and soul, it has never been more important to seek the help of love. We have the words of St John the Divine to still our doubts: 'There is no fear in love but perfect love casteth out fear.'

Living fully

To live fully. To be fully alive. The words, the concept, have always attracted me with a kind of fearful thrill: fearful because, burdened, as I suppose we all are, with the weight of caution engendered in us throughout our childhood, the weight of 'do nots' were always there to curtail any ecstacy-threatening moments hanging about: swinging, for instance, to great heights on branches or careering dizzily down homemade slides in frosty weather. Living fully, with mind, heart and senses gloriously coordinated, seemed also to be living dangerously – and that was bad!

I think many of us shrink more and more away from living fully: we might get hurt; we might give too much away; it's safer, more prudent, to live within parameters we have judiciously fashioned for ourselves: a neat and ordered framework rigorously maintained; walls meticulously built, boulder upon boulder, stone upon stone – always keeping a vigilant eye out for any gaps which might appear and which have to be mended immediately lest something unpleasant gains entry to our carefully tilled patch. And so we maintain our lives with care and due caution; nothing gets in and nothing goes out.

I have just lost a friend to death; a friend who lived her life fully. She was a teacher who loved her students and her subject. She loved people and laughter. She loved truth and beauty. She loved energy and effort. The created world was filled with wonders for her. She was fearless in her condemnation of anything and everything that offended against God's design for us. She built no walls about herself and recognised no walls about others. Her generosity of spirit was unbounded; her warmth of heart encircled all, making no distinction between classes or creeds. Her sense of fun was a joy to us all. She lived fully, was fully alive right up to the moment of her death. Her favourite poem was John Donne's 'Death, be not Proud' so, for Brigid, whose gift for living fully has transcended her death, here it is:

Death, be not proud, though some have called thee
Mighty and dreadful, for thou art not so:
For those, whom thou think'st thou dost overthrow
Die not, poor Death; nor yet canst thou kill me.
From Rest and Sleep, which but thy pictures be,
Much pleasure, then from thee much more must flow;
And soonest with thee our best men do go –
Rest of their bones, and souls' delivery!
Thou'rt slave to Fate, Chance, kings, and desperate men,
And dost with poison, war, and sickness dwell;
And poppy or charms can make us sleep as well
And better than thy stroke. Why swell'st thou then!
One short sleep past, we wake eternally,
And Death shall be no more: Death, thou shalt die!

Light a candle

My mother, God rest her, was a woman of sayings: she had a saying for almost every occasion, dilemma, event – most of which were incomprehensible to me as a child in terms of their philosophical or cautionary content, but all of which had the comfort of familiarity. And so I would nod away happily when she would utter, in response to a friend's extravagant scheme, 'You must cut your coat according to your cloth' or in response to another's stubborn pessimism, 'Ah, the blind man sees all the world dark'.

'Self-praise is no praise,' she might say, if she heard me waxing fulsome about the merits of an essay I had just written. I understood that one, and didn't like it one bit. Some of her sayings were in Irish and translated rather flabbily into, 'It takes one to know one!' and, 'If you lie down with dogs don't be surprised when you get up with fleas!'. I thought this last one was a bit strong when it was issued darkly in relation to a brand-new friend I had made. I was fourteen and my exotic new friend had suspiciously red lips and sometimes wore HIGH HEELS! TO MASS! I discovered later that the high heels were being spirited unbenownst out of her mother's wardrobe, and the scarlet lips came from a particular religious magazine. This magazine had a red cover, and my new friend had made a serendipitous discovery, involving an accident with a cup of tea, that the red colour, when wet, came off on your hands. 'Holy lipstick,' she announced with gleeful irreverence, and I shivered with fearful excitement.

But I digress. My mother and her sayings are on my mind because, recently, I overheard one of her favourites being given breath during a gathering of friends. My heart leaped with the joy of recognition and I experienced a powerful, involuntary sense of my mother's presence.

'There are those who curse the darkness, and there are those who light a candle.' The words resounded in the depths of my being. Dear God, I thought, as I drove home, let me be a lighter of candles. I have cursed the darkness often enough and for long enough. I thought of the insidious power that the darkness of famine, inhumanity, violence, injustice and our failures has to trap us in despair. We blunder about, stumbling and cutting ourselves on jagged obstacles we cannot see, grateful when someone lights a candle but unable to light one of our own. What does it take to light a candle? Faith! Yes, faith that what will be revealed is the other side of darkness: the light of the divine in humankind; the light of courage, love, decency and generosity of mind and spirit. And the more candles we light, the more the divine will be revealed and the fainter will become the cries of those who can only curse the darkness.

71

Miracle of Lourdes

That year, the part of France in which we were staying with friends was only a couple of hours away from Lourdes, and we all agreed that a trip was in order. The day we had chosen to travel there was one of the hottest we had experienced since arriving. A molten sun beat down mercilessly, scorching the air about us, leaving us limp and exhausted; and filling my head, at least, with a dazed longing for cool Irish streams, for blessed, fresh, Irish rain.

And Lourdes! Lourdes was instantly disappointing. I had never been there before and I had expected to feel ... I don't know ... something ... some sense of the holiness of the place ... a strange charge, perhaps, in the atmosphere ... something ... anything to indicate that this was a special place, a place apart, a place that enabled one to transcend the limitations of ordinary experience.

Instead, I found myself resenting everything: the suffocating heat, the crowds, the noise, the shops and stalls, the haggling and chattering, the smells of food which were making my stomach lurch sickeningly. Like a disappointed child I wanted to go home immediately.

We went to the Grotto but I could feel nothing, just a huge

lump in my throat that kept threatening to choke me. Time passed in a hot, dizzying swirl of noise, shapes and colours; I dimly heard someone say that the procession of the sick had started.

I could hear the sound of voices raised in song and then the sick came into view; some walking, some in wheelchairs, some on stretchers – so many sick and suffering humans. I saw faces gaunt and emaciated; I saw bodies shrivelled and wasted. I heard prayers uttered in many different tongues. I saw beseeching eyes, supplicating hands; above all, I witnessed a strength of noble courage of a kind I had never witnessed so powerfully before.

The air about me now was charged with compassion and love, with an almost unbearable tenderness. The holiness of the place settled about me for the first time – a holiness borne out of the gift of human suffering offered over and over to God with faith and hope and love.

I became aware that the lump in my throat had dissolved and that tears were coursing down my face. I felt my soul rise to be at one with the suffering and I felt the healing deep in my heart's core.

The hard road

Mary must have felt fearful sometimes on that hard road to
Bethlehem, the child moving strongly within her, knowing
about the pain lying in wait for her. As she neared her
destination she must also have felt a growing sense of awe.
And even when she leaned against Joseph's comforting
weight, even when she gratefully accepted his steadying arm
about her, she must have found herself withdrawing into a
place quintessentially female; a place where the powerful
contractions of pain are suffered and exchanged for the
awesome mystery of life; a place where the relentless,
excruciating, emptying of the womb fills beseeching arms
with the infant human face of need and love; a place where
joy is hard-won and wholly deserved.

There do not appear to be any other women in the stable
with her – and I find myself wondering why this should be
so. I feel sure they were there with her during her time of
need: the owner's wife, mother, sister! I feel sure the gentle,
insistent urgings of women, their cool hands, their strong
arms, were there to see her through. Their hearts would
have gone out to her, their sister in travail, so young! 'It will
soon be over, little one,' they would have said. 'Just bear
with it a little longer and it will be over.' A strong, tender
female world of knowledge holding her close, seeing her

through. 'You have a son,' they would have cried later. 'You have a beautiful, strong, healthy boy!' And they would have stroked her sweat-tangled hair and told her how brave she had been, so brave for a young lass of sixteen.

As Mary held her infant son that first time, did she feel the cold steel breath of the sword that would one day pierce both their souls? Did she have an inkling that this child to whom she had given a heartbeat, to whom during years of loving care she would give eyes to see the lilies of the field, a voice the people of the world would hear for evermore in the silence of their souls, this child on whom she would lavish so much, would one day be wrenched from her life and broken in pieces by hatred.

I see Mary in every mother following after a hearse. I hear her in every mother's prayer to take away our hearts of stone and give us hearts of flesh and blood. Her heart shares the frightened beat of every mother's heart who hears the knock on the door in the middle of the night, the sound of gunfire, the sickening reverberations of an explosion. Her heart quails, threatens to fail, like ours, when we look on the terrifying inhuman face of blind conviction.

It is the hard road Mary shares with us, the hard road when there is no wind on our backs; the same hard road she walked herself in faith, hope and love – to the end is faith, hope and love.

Chains of nostalgia

Sheltered, when the rain blew over the hills it was, sunny
all day when the days of summer were long. Beyond all
rumour of labouring towns it was. But at dawn and
evening its trees were noisy with song.

Nostalgic opening lines of a poem by J.C. Squires that
resonate warmly in my head and heart; don't we all
remember with a sweet painful yearning the summers of
our youth that stretched before us like endless rivers of joy?
And don't we remember with the same yearning how
sheltered from the biting winds and rain of winter we were
as children, warm in our beds, our feet playing
contentedly, if gingerly, with the socked hot-water jar;
hearts and minds soothed by the low murmur of familiar
voices drifting upwards from the kitchen below? Don't you
remember?

And don't we all yearn for the simplicity, the integrity, of
that first world we knew, its beautiful certainties, its clear
lines, its firm, steadfast boundaries; a world lost to us, the
memory of which serves to darken today's world as shoddy,
rootless, violent, threatening?

Isn't it that yearning for a time gone by that has us scrambling to read sentimental accounts of golden-age children running barefoot to school through the fields, waving goodbye to mothers leaning rosy-faced over the half-door, shouting greetings to singing birds and bleating lambs, crushing ripe blackberries to their sticky, innocent mouths?

Nostalgia: a sentimental yearning for the past. Recently, I read an account by a young woman who had been a heroin addict. In it she claimed a strong link between her addiction and nostalgia: she yearned obsessively for that first high she had experienced with the drug; her years of addiction, she wrote, were bound up in her attempts to reproduce that first high. She now saw nostalgia as an enemy that had kept her chained to the past, alienated from the present, blind to the future. To all intents and purposes, she had been, she said, a dead thing. To live again, she had to free herself from the chains of nostalgia.

In the words of Bhagwan Shree Rajneesh:

> There is only one courage and that is the courage to go on dying to the past, not to collect it, not to accumulate it, not to cling to it. We all cling to the past, and because we cling to the past we become unavailable to the present.

Comfort zones

There was a group of us together one day and one of us
told a story about a person we all knew that revealed her in
a warm, generous and compassionate light. 'I wish you
hadn't told that story,' a member of the group said crossly.
'I've always enjoyed disliking her and now you've ruined it
for me. I'm going to pretend I never heard that story.' And
this from one who loves music and spring, who waxes
poetic at sunsets. And in her reluctance to change her mind
she has plenty of company: the person who weeps before
the beauty of the dawn, a miracle of transformation, can
also be the one who clings stubbornly to old convictions,
bitter assessments; the person who traces with wonder the
journey of the butterfly from caterpillar to bright, delicate,
winged beauty, can also set his face grimly against a change
of heart.

The world about us is a miracle of constant change, a
miracle of transformation, renewal, growth. A young girl I
once sat beside on a bus journey told me that her beloved
grandmother, as she lay dying, was asked by one of her
daughters if there was anything at all she wanted. The old
woman smiled and nodded towards the window and
whispered, 'I've just been given the only thing I asked for.'
Her daughter glanced up to discover the whole sky

illuminated by a rainbow. 'You wished for a rainbow?' her daughter asked in wonder and her mother nodded, smiled again and closed her eyes.

The most fascinating human stories are those that tell of lives liberated through transformation – and yet we often hold fast to our own comfort zones of hard conviction, old hatreds and prejudices, iron-cladding them about us and calling the house we build with them, 'Steadfast'.

But while we marvel at the miracles of change happening around us, there is still hope for our hearts – as there was for the seventeeth-century poet, George Herbert:

> Who would have thought my shrivel'd heart
> Could have recovered greennesse
> ....
> And now in age I bud again,
> After so many deaths I live and write;
> I once more smell the dew and rain.
>
> FROM 'THE FLOWER' BY GEORGE HERBERT

I hope you dance

It was only recently, more than a year after my friend, Lorna, had lost her long battle with illness, that I felt able at last to seek out and pore over old photographs and letters – testaments to our friendship. Before that, a chance encounter with a photograph showing her radiant face, or a note in her tiny, neat handwriting would send my heart lurching sickeningly in my chest with the weight of her loss. How could someone so full of grace and courage and light have slipped away from us so quietly? From her husband, her family, her friends? How could we have lost her so hopelessly, so completely? For me, the desolate void created by her absence for a time became infected with bitter thoughts of wickedness prospering while grace and goodness were laid low. Bleak, bleak, days.

Now, at least, I could look at photographs and read notes that plucked the strings of my memory and smile again as her infectious enthusiasm for life tumbled off the pages. And then I remembered the poem; the poem about dancing that Lorna had sent me after she had returned home from a visit to us during which we had celebrated non-stop what had appeared to be, at last, her hard-won triumph over her illness.

'I hope you dance!' That was it! That was the name of the poem – and the title had echoed as a refrain throughout. I searched feverishly for the poem. I couldn't remember any lines – just the gist of it; through darkness and light, through pain and joy, through winter and summer, I hope you dance, I hope you dance.

On a summer beach, my tiny granddaughter throws her arms wide as if to embrace the sea and, in a breathtaking configuration of leaps, whirls and swoops, dances her ecstasy to an audience of waves and gulls. I hope you dance.

In a theatre in Belfast on a cold winter's night we are invited to watch the dancer soar to impossible heights, and deep in our heart's core we know that we are indeed, dancer and watcher, touched by the Divine. I hope you dance.

The soul sings, the spirit soars, the heart dances. Summer dances to the still, contemplative heart of winter; spring dances to the sweet courage of autumn. I hope you dance.

I hope you dance in the heart of suffering, in the darkness and the pain; that is where the most beautiful, because they are the most life affirming, dances of all are created. I hope you dance.

I hope you dance to ease the loneliness of another, to celebrate a new dawn, to say goodbye. I remember that at the end of her letter, which contained the poem, Lorna wrote: 'I know you dance.'

I hope I do. I hope I do.

Leave room for redemption

Recently, on television, I listened to a poet explain the reason why the hymn, 'Amazing Grace', holds a significant place in his heart. The composer, he told us, had been a slave-owner who had awakened one morning clad in the saving knowledge that his way of life was wrong and that he could no longer be a part of the evil that was slavery. He had composed the hymn as a celebration of the transformational grace with which he had been gifted on that blessed morning.

The poet, whose own forebears were victims of slavery, quoted words from out of his generous heart: 'We must always,' he said, 'leave room for redemption.' In truth, the poet hadn't always been left that room for redemption himself. Having suffered a hard, abusive childhood, as a young adult he had gravitated towards the kind of anti-social, petty-criminal behaviour that seemed to offer some ease to his angry and resentful heart. Later, he discovered, through poetry, a love of learning and the truth of his own being. Sadly there were those who were blind to the amazing redemptive grace with which he had been blessed and who used his past against him in crippling ways.

When I was a twelve-year-old schoolgirl and, according to

my mother, as wild as a March hare, I was at the centre of
an incident involving a runaway bicycle, two flights of stairs
and an innocent nun who ended up under the wheels of the
aforementioned bike. The incident was the result of a dare
tossed at me carelessly by a schoolmate but the trouble I
got into afterwards dogged me for what seemed like
forever. Regardless of all my efforts to redeem myself, I was
only ever known as the one who'd cycled down two flights
of stairs at breakneck speed on the caretaker's bicycle – and
oh horrors! – had run over a nun in the process. In the end
it was the victim of my caper herself who saved me: she
came to me one day and suggested with a smile that, in
effect, I deserved to be left room for redemption. And she
ensured in various subtly effective ways that others left me
the same room. Her creative response to my youthful plight
ensured that, many, many years later, I became a liberal
dispenser of clean slates to my own students. And woe
betide any colleague who, well-intentioned or otherwise,
looked over my shoulder at the beginning of a school year
and, pointing at my new class-list, said: 'Clamp down on
that one from the very start. I had her last year and she had
my heart broken.'

A leopard may not change its spots but every human being
open to redemptive grace can rebirth himself miraculously.
When we refuse to leave room for redemption we blind
ourselves to the power of that amazing grace.

Surprised by joy

Surprised by joy – impatient as the Wind
I turned to share the transport – Oh! With who but
Thee.

FROM 'SURPRISED BY JOY' BY WILLIAM WORDSWORTH

Beautiful lines by William Wordsworth that convey both
the suddenness with which we are often visited by joy, and
the irresistible human need we have to share the ecstasy
with someone we love. Wordsworth's joy is short-lived
because in his joyful transport, he has forgotten that she
with whom he is impatient to share the moment is no more,
and with the renewed shocked realisation of his 'most
grievous loss' he suffers the

worst pang that someone ever bore,
Save one, one only, when I stood forlorn,
Knowing my heart's best treasure was no more;
That neither present time, nor years unborn
Could to my sight that heavenly face restore.

Recently, we travelled to the West of Ireland to attend the
funeral of a beautiful young man: a son, a husband, a father,
a friend, whose death was shocking in its suddenness, and in
the dazed, bewildered grief it left in its wake. We returned

84

home to hear news of another death; this time of a woman in the mature summer of her life, a warm, loving, creative woman with a beautiful, smiling face; a wife, a mother, a sister, a friend. In a matter of days the world I knew had lost two people it could ill afford to lose; two people whose generous, loving lives turned their deaths into aching irreplaceable loss.

On the day between the two funerals, I listened to an elderly man speak about his sixty years in the priesthood. He had been speculating, he said, about whether or not he had acquired any wisdom worth imparting at this stage of his life, and he had decided that, yes, he had: we should seek out and embrace joy in our lives, he said. We blind ourselves to the shining face of joy, he said, because we are afraid. Our courage fails us in the face of pain, anxiety, grief and we become more comfortable with joylessness. And yet, the brave faith-filled heart easily accommodates both joy and sorrow, embracing one through knowledge of the other.

It is a surprising thought, isn't it? It is faith and courage we need to be truly joyful.

My perfect angel

'You are my perfect angel,' I told my three-year-old granddaughter at Christmas.

'Yes, I know,' she responded happily, taking the time to come to a halt in mid-pirouette. She fluffed out the tulle skirt of her Halloween fairy costume with which she had insisted on gracing Christmas Day. 'And,' she continued, finishing her pirouette, 'do you know that I'm probably the best girl in the whole world and everybody loves me because I'm very good as well at singing and smiling.' To illustrate her great giftedness she smiled brilliantly for the duration of at least thirty seconds, after which she treated me to an enthusiastic version of 'I Had a Little Nut-Tree'.

Later as we worked on a jigsaw together, I covertly studied her perfectly beautiful little face with its expression of rapt concentration, and the thought that she might ever feel less cherished, less gifted, less like an angel than she feels now saddened me immeasurably.

How do we travel so far from that bright place of knowledge of our own lovableness, our own goodness, and end up lost in that darker place where often we are conscious only of our inadequacies, our unworthiness? And, sadly, the more lost we become to the goodness of ourselves the more lost we become to the truth of a loving God.

Once during a fairly frivolous discussion on auras – the invisible emanation that, it is believed, surrounds the bodies of all living creatures and that some people claim to be able to see and read in relation to the subjects' mental, physical and spiritual health – one of those present said to me quite seriously, 'You know, Mary, I saw your aura one time and it was beautiful – peaceful and benign.' Accurate or not, serious or in jest, her words filled me with inexplicable gratitude. Was it possible that, despite years of living uneasily under the shadow of my failings, that I was really a good person with a beautiful aura?! Embedded in my unexpected response was a feeling that I had been in some way miraculously returned to myself. I had been lost and now was found. Amazing grace, indeed.

The poet, Wordsworth, writes about the child trailing clouds of glory as he comes from God 'who is our home'. Gradually, according to the poet, the world shapes a prison house around the growing child and his sense of his glory dims.

My three-year-old granddaughter still trails her clouds of glory. Surely she, and every other child in the world, has a right never to be imprisoned in a house of unworthiness, never to be separated from the knowledge of her own trailing clouds of glory.

Manners!

The other day I found myself walking behind a young teenager. He was dressed in a neat school uniform and was noisily munching crisps while guzzling a fizzy drink from a tin. I was genuinely shocked when he casually threw his empty crisp bag and tin over a garden wall, onto someone's lawn.

'Aw, come on now, young fellow,' I said, good-humouredly to his back. 'Why did you do that? I think you should go back and collect your rubbish from that garden and put it in the nearest bin!'

He turned round and trained his young blue eyes on me and with undisguised contempt and in the foulest language, he told me what he thought of my suggestion. I literally reeled back as if I had been physically struck; shocked tears sprang to my eyes. I read recently that new scientific research maintains that the brain reacts to a social insult in the same way as it does to a physical injury – and I can well believe it.

The previous day I had stubbornly refused to accept my change from a sales assistant even though she kept waggling it impatiently in my direction. She, herself, you see, was turned in another direction, animatedly engaged in a conversation with a colleague. For her, I simply did not exist.

The soul shrivels, the heart shrinks, the body recoils before the knife-edge of contempt. And contempt it is that appears to have routed ordinary human decency and courtesy – the decency and courtesy we used to call good manners. I truly believe with all my heart that contempt felt for and displayed towards another is a denial of the other's soul, of the Divine within, indeed, of God.

We are all guilty. Tabloids explode people's lives; politicians hurtle insults at each other; open season has been declared on public figures; motorists scream obscenities at each other; individualism of the worst kind is rife; monstrous egos are forever on parade.

Small children's wondering, sensuous apprehension of the natural world about them is a miracle to behold; what kind of world have we created that clears so effectively the wonder from the child's eyes and replaces it with cruel indifference? What disrespectful words of ours, of mine, gave birth to that young fellow's contempt? And the young sales assistant for whom I didn't exist! What affliction of indifference has she experienced that enables her to deny the existence of others.

When we sow the seeds of disrespect, of egotism, in a contemptuous mockery of spring, the crop we reap in autumn can be an ugly one.

Balance

For me, one of the most profoundly beautiful words in the English language is the word 'balance'. It touches something deep within my soul; something which longs for an ideal state of being. Someone once said our love of symmetry, balance, is a reflection of our own innate satisfaction with our own two arms and legs. True, perhaps, but too exclusively bound up with the ego to be all of the truth.

It is to the soul, I believe, as it journeys through this world of contraries, that the concept of balance appeals most, because the ultimate balance must be to draw the contraries in our own natures together on the ground of love, to see the contraries in the world about us: love and fear, war and peace, greed and altruism, bitterness and forgiveness, brought together with charity and compassion, transformed by love.

Two weddings I attended recently were miracles of balance. The first was the wedding of a young couple from different cultural, racial and religious backgrounds: the bride, Irish, Christian; the groom Indian, Hindu.

The Christian service was graced by a beautiful Hindu marriage prayer. Later in the hotel on a balcony overlooking the bright sea, the Holy Man conducting the Hindu ceremony explained everything that was happening with clarity, depth and an unexpected twinkling humour. The bride was dazzling in white; the bridesmaids glowed in rich, ceremonial red. There was a two-hour stint of Céili dancing at which all and sundry kicked up their heels. Balance reigned.

The second wedding I thought would break my heart. The bride was the daughter of a dear friend, a soul-friend, who had lost her long battle with illness six months before. My friend was lovely and loving, a shining spirit filled with laughter and an unflinching courage. I said I thought this wedding would break my heart; instead, I came away with a quiet, peaceful heart because, throughout the day, joy and grief, hearts filled with love and hope and hearts aching with longing for what might have been came together in natural balance. I saw the dancer's soaring leap; the greening of winter, the darkness making way for the dawn; life and earth meeting to celebrate the power of love, the endurance of the soul and the ever-onward march of hope.

Balance is all.

The burgeoning spirit
and the declining body

I was standing in a supermarket checkout queue the other day gazing idly at the back of what I took to be an eighteen-year-old or thereabouts female. Size 8, I thought, with what might have been an envious sigh; certainly no more than a size 10 – but she'll get a cold in her kidneys in that get-up! The girl's midriff was bare. She was wearing one of those designer shrunk tops and hipster jeans – a fashion, I thought primly, so antithetical to our chilly climes as to be asking for trouble of a medical nature.

The 'girl' turned around to claim her trolley and I realised she was not a girl at all – she was a woman well advanced into her forties. I suddenly felt drained of everything except sadness. Why was this woman dressed as though she were her own teenage daughter? Was it because she'd given in to the modern world's insistence that youth, and youth alone, is to be valued, celebrated, desired.

Had she dieted herself into a size 8 and opted for the dubious youthful craze for small clothes (and kidney infections) in order to be in favour! Was there a size 14+ with a fondness for elasticated waistbands and full-fat dairy produce bursting to reveal herself – or was that just me standing behind her!

It used to be that youth was indulged resignedly, smiled at, admired, certainly, for its beauty – but not revered, not adored, not desperately clung to. Its brevity was acknowledged, its passing was mourned – but a lifetime in which the spirit continues to burgeon lay ahead; a lifetime for the acquisition of necessary wisdom, for the maturing of the mind, for the ego to give way to the soul; a lifetime to be embraced fully. Out of that lifetime of suffering and joy was forged the gift of wisdom for old age.

The lazy, lovely days of youth are charged with distraction, but wisdom lies in letting go. A society that venerates only youth makes it into a cult, diminishes, even endangers it; age treats the miraculous journey of the soul with contempt. Why, then, when I know this, do I sometimes long to be twenty years younger and several sizes slimmer? Ah, frailty!

Stranded on an alien shore

Recently I spent a couple of weeks in bed with a serious bout of summer flu – or whatever it is the medical profession calls a combination of aching bones, high temperature and paroxysms of coughing to beat the band, symptoms, incidentally, surely better suited to the icy depths of winter. I lay marooned on my bed, weak, vulnerable, painfully conscious, as you only are when you believe yourself to be terminally ill, of how dependent we humans are for our continued existence on the successful functioning of a rickle of bones, a variety of fleshy organs and some complicated circulatory highway systems. One significant glitch in the works, I thought, and the me in whom I have invested so much, the me of whom, over the years, I have become quite fond, the me who loves the garden of her life more and more with each passing year, may go out like a light. Here one moment, gone the next!

Friends came on tentative visits from the planet Health, looking more than usually red-cheeked and robust. They moved through my bedroom doorway and said things like, 'You look awful; what have you been doing to yourself!' As they left I could hear the door to the banqueting room slamming shut against me. I felt excluded, isolated; voices became distant; life was happening in other rooms.

As I lay one morning drenched in perspiration, having hallucinated a nightmare journey through the night, I was struck by the conviction that the greatest distance exists, not between the living and the dead, but between the sick and the healthy. The sick lie stranded on a bleak and lonely shore, oceans distant from the bright, sunlit sands on which the healthy feast and dance. And across the oceans that divide them, the healthy turn their eyes away, hide behind swirling mists of denial, evasiveness; reluctant to let the shadow of mortality fall across their feasting and dancing. And the bleak shore on which the sick lie stranded grows darker and more lonely; the oceans between the worlds swell; the sounds and voices of the healthy grow dim.

We are enjoined to visit the sick. We need to enter their world with compassion, with courage and imagination, for it is in the sickroom that we bridge distance, look deeply into our own eyes, embrace fear with warm arms and ease the loneliness of us all, sick and healthy.

Gifts of words and gifts of silence

Paul is married to one of my oldest and dearest friends. She has often said she fell in love with his generous heart first, followed swiftly by his wonderful way with words. And indeed Paul's lifelong relationship with words has been a passionate and reverent one.

Wittgenstein said: 'The limits of my language means the limits of my world.' Paul would have agreed with this. He would have agreed that our understanding of the world, of ourselves, would be sadly limited without the language that defines, articulates, elaborates. Paul's passionate reverence for language meant that he never threw words away idly; his discourse was a miracle of lucidity and precision. He had the poetic gift for a well-wrought metaphor, the perfect allusion. I never heard him utter a gratuitously bitter word or a foul word. I never heard him swear. His generous heart and mind and his use of language blended together harmoniously as one.

Some years ago, Paul suffered a stroke, and one of the cruel legacies of that stroke was the loss of his language. I don't understand why this should have happened to a man who had such reverence for the gift of language; to a man who, to my knowledge, never abused language, never threw words like stones to cut people and make them bleed. I, who share his love for language, had no words for him then to explain why he had been silenced. God knows. We hear people every day in the marketplace, in the media, whose language is bitter, hate-filled, foul and blasphemous. They have not been silenced. We hear people, under the guise of religious fervour, preach hatred and division; we hear torrents of lies from the rich, the powerful, the manipulative. They have not been silenced. We hear ourselves speak words that hurt and deride, alienate and frighten. We have not been silenced.

If Paul's silence has meaning, and I believe it does, then it speaks of the miracle of words; of the reverence we should have for the naming of things; of the burden of responsibility we bear each time we open our mouths to speak.

Paul's good soul still shines out of his eyes. What meanings are we making out of our mouths? And what meanings are we teaching our children to make out of theirs?

A heavy heart

Weight creeps up on me like a perverse thief in the night; perverse, because this thief is putting stuff back, instead of stealing it away. One day I'm stepping along lightly in a neat middle-size 12; the next I'm clumping heavily about, railing against the nocturnal villain who plastered two sizes on me as I lay innocently sleeping.

That's one kind of weight I will always be carrying around with me to some degree or another; but, secretly, I discovered I was carrying a different kind of tonnage around. You know the way disparate things come together sometimes? Strands of conversations about forgiveness, related ponderings and readings suddenly gravitated towards one another and shaped coherently into a rather startling revelation: something I thought I had long forgiven a dearly loved friend, forgotten in fact, had instead lain hidden in a cold, dark, place of my mind; unforgiven, unforgotten.

In the wake of the revelation came rushing the answer to a question I had often asked myself over the years: why did, at best, irritation, and, at worst, illogical anger, so often inform my relationship with this dear friend? Now I understand.

The need to put things right was immediate and insistent. The fear of saying the wrong thing, of making things worse, of being misunderstood, rejected, causing confusion, almost caused my courage to fail at the last moment. However, with a silent plea heavenwards for grace, I managed to communicate my discovery to my friend, whose response was instant and full of grace: 'What a terrible weight that must have been for you to carry around all these years!'

And that is what unforgiveness is, make no mistake about it: a terrible insidious weight that creeps up on you like a thief in the night, dulling your compassion, crushing your spontaneity, clogging your system with fatty deposits of anger and resentment, inexplicable irritation, robbing your relationships of clarity and light.

Light broke over my friend's head and she emerged from the shadows my unforgiving heart had created for her. Now I could see her clearly: a loyal, loving, trusting, good friend; broken as we all are; seeking healing, completion, as we all are. Good, loving friend.

To be known

Look at me! Look at meeee! Everyone seems to be screaming demands to be looked at these days. A far cry from the lass who

> dwelt among the untrodden ways
> Beside the springs of Dove,
> A Maid whom there were no to praise
> And very few to love.
>
> FROM 'LUCY POEMS' BY WILLIAM WORDSWORTH

Wordsworth's modest Lucy; his 'violet by a mossy stone/Half-hidden from the eye!' who was content to live out her days in rustic anonymity. I thought of her the other day while I listened to a radio discussion on the cult of celebrity. A panel, itself made up of well-known people, talked about the lengths to which others are prepared to go in order to be known and the abysmal depths to which the rest of us are prepared to plummet in order to know them; these celebrities without portfolio.

We all need to be known by at least one other person in order to believe that we exist. Wordsworth's Lucy was known by the great poet himself; known and loved, immortalised in verse, no less.

To be unknown is to be a shadow – or to feel like a shadow. Our desire for celebrity, for fame, is because we suspect that we might not fully exist unless we are acknowledged by someone other than ourselves. All that struggle to be known, all that willingness of people to humiliate themselves publicly on television; all that appalling, attention-grabbing behaviour of would-be celebrities, is just a more shrill, more desperate than normal cry for the world's reassurance that they exist.

The rich and powerful do it; politicians do it; stars and wannabe stars do it; the rest of us do it in our own way, sometimes subtly, sometimes obviously; children do it all the time. Aggressively or in plaintive whispers, we all seek to be known. When we mock the Jades and the Johnnies we mock our own need to be known. We are fascinated by people's thirst for celebrity because if offers, in a distorting mirror, perhaps an image of our own need or acknowledgement.

Unfortunately, we seek reassurance that we are not shadows from people like ourselves who need the same reassurances. We empower others to give us what we crave, but both the empowerment and the acknowledgement we get in return are without substance.

The fortunate ones, the truly blessed, are those who answer their heart's need to be known by seeking that need's fulfilment from the God of Love. They are the real achievers of glory; they, and they alone, are the truly known.

Betrayal

When it was evening, Jesus and the twelve disciples sat
down to eat. During the meal, Jesus said, 'I tell you, one
of you will betray me.'

MATTHEW 26:20-22

'Betrayal': the very word strikes deep into our hearts, laying
bare old wounds preserved in outrage. Which of us cannot
remember the sting of that first betrayal by someone in
whom we had innocently placed our trust? I remember.
The years, much to my mortification, have not remotely
diffused the memory, or the shock, of my first betrayal by
someone I trusted. My very best school friend, I
discovered, had been making fun of my home-knit jumpers
behind my back. Of course, I was well aware that my
mother wasn't the western world's best knitter, but, on the
other hand, my sense of sartorial elegance wasn't very
highly developed so, with careless indifference to the figure
I cut, I had rolled up the too-long sleeve out of the way and
stuck a safety pin in the too-wide neckband. My mother
knitted for us with love; my father and I wore her inelegant
creations with a reciprocal love.

The discovery that my friend, who had gorged every
Tuesday on my mother's perfect apple cakes and potato

bread, had betrayed us both, stole innocence and trust from me. For an act of betrayal to pierce shockingly home, there has to have been trust beforehand. When trust is breached, innocence is ruptured at the same time; two precious birthrights damaged forever.

We are far distant from first betrayals and have become used to a world in which cynicism is a popular currency; trust in power and authority is eroded daily. We almost expect to be betrayed by those who govern us, by those who seek to have influence and authority over our minds, our bodies, our hearts and our souls. And that is sad. The hopelessness of it deadens our spirits. We long to be able to believe in the innate goodness of humankind and in the benign intentions of those who have power over our lives. We long for a return to that first world of innocence and trust, a world blessed by the poet William Blake, where children and lambs gambol in green, sunlit pastures.

But, do you know, my world tilted on me the other day with the force of a line from another poet: 'We are betrayed by what is false within.' That was the line that came into my head unbidden. It is not the betrayals of others which are the most killing; it is the falseness, the lies we wilfully or ignorantly harbour within us which create the most deadly and deadening betrayals of all.

The gift of new sight to the blind:
A Christmas reflection

The child was born in the darkness of a stable at Bethlehem and at his birth the world was flooded with light and the light was the love of God. And among the long-promised gifts emerging from the light of the child's birth was the gift of new sight to the blind. And this gift of new sight to the blind is for all and forever: a miraculous illuminating gift which new-washes our eyes so that we can see love in all things.

Why do we turn away, confused, dazzled by the light of the gift? Why do we cling to the dark walls of our own rage, our hatreds, our loathing for a world which seems to frustrate our longings at every turn? If we only see what is visible and if what is visible only fills us with despair or a raging need for vengeance, then we have not accepted the gift of new sight. Because the gift of new sight, born with the Christ Child, illuminates the love in all things and lets us see the cruel, the murderous, the oppressor, the greedy, for what they are: the brokenness of a love which has become ill.

There is a dark, dark place that lives in each of us, a frightened, lonely place which cries to us in the night. To accept the gift of new sight is to illuminate that dark, lonely place within and reveal it to us as an inner chamber where the knowledge of love resides. As the blind, we turn outwards to answer the cry that comes from within. 'Behold I stand at the door and knock. If anyone hears my voice and opens the door I will go in and sup with him and he with me.'

'And to the blind new sight' – Isaiah's promise from God gathered light through the ages until it flamed into fulfilment at Bethlehem, penetrating the darkness of a stable, illuminating the face of a new-born child who is the fulfilment of that promise: the giver of new sight to the blind.

We are the blind whose eyes are made whole through the knowledge of divine love, whose dark is illuminated, enabling us to see through and beyond what is merely visible to the unloving eye.

To see that there is light in all darkness.

To see with the gift of new sight.

The gift withheld

Two thousand years ago a child was born into the world, a child whose naked need for his mother's breast, for his father's loving shade, rendered all the more awesome the power he held within him to teach humankind how to live.

'A baby small is come to teach.' As his mother holds him in her arms, he holds in his beating heart a message of love that holds within it the gift of wisdom, wisdom to set free the minds, hearts and imaginations of every woman and man. What a holding is there! A gift of wisdom held within the embrace of a mother's arms and a father's loving shade! I spoke the other day to a group of children: a group of 14-year-old girls. I said, 'If you had a magic wand this Christmas, what would you magic into being?' One child said, with a weight of concern in her voice, that she would mend the holes in the ozone layer because they were giving her 'wild bad dreams' at night. Another said she would bring peace to Northern Ireland. And so it went on: food for the hungry, who haunted them; love for the world's doomed children; healing for our endangered polluted planet. And I thought, what have we done to our own children? Their hearts are heavy with anxiety. Their dreams are filled with nightmare images of sick, starving babies, rumours of war, messages of bigotry and hate. The very earth on which they should be playing joyfully seems to be cracking and splitting under their feet.

What a failure of love is there! And they know it. They are wise and sad beyond their years. They told me that, yes, they know too about the triumphs of love in the world; about the hearts and minds and imaginations touched by love, the spirits set free and soaring beyond patch-bound greed, bigotry, fever and fret. In their own lives they have experienced care and nurture, laughter and tenderness. But they wonder why the world's 'bad guys' are so powerful, so seemingly unstoppable. And they are frightened.

Our children, this Christmas, will receive gifts of trains and dolls, woolly mufflers and furry boots. They are owed more, much more.

Two thousand years ago a child was born into the world, a child who held within his beating heart, a precious gift of wisdom for humankind, a gift of wisdom held within a simple message of love. It is the fruits of that wisdom we owe to our children. When are we going to give them the gift of quiet dreams and good clean earth to play upon? How long will we continue to withhold the gift?

Christmas found

A friend of mine thought she had lost Christmas one year. She and her husband were living and working in East Africa when the child they were expecting decided to begin her launch into their unsuspecting world very early on Christmas morning. In the wake of unmistakable signs of their daughter's decision lay an endless nightmare drive through unfamiliar terrain, very different from the rolling landscape of my friend's native County Derry. They arrived at last at a primitive hospital, which was deserted by all save one nurse. There followed a difficult birth and a fragile, vulnerable new life. And my friend in her weariness thought sadly of the tinsel gathering dust back in their bungalow; of the presents lying unopened; the food mouldering; Christmas fading: the wasting of all her efforts to reproduce the warm familiarity of an Irish Christmas here in the frighteningly beautiful East African landscape.

Six months later, holding her precious daughter (who had miraculously survived a very dangerous infancy) my friend found herself thinking about that lost Christmas. She thought of the decimation of all her careful plans when out of the clear blue African sky she experienced a joyful realisation: she had not lost Christmas six months before – rather she had found Christmas.

She had, in fact, touched the very heart of Christmas because what is at the heart of Christmas is as human as it is divine. What was at the heart of that first Christmas was human pain, fear, confusion, unfamiliar surroundings, birth, blood and joy. It was when God was revealed, not as remote and coldly judgemental of human frailty, but truly as a God of love, a God willing to share our humanness. There were so many ways that God could have chosen to manifest his face to the world. He chose to share and thereby affirm our humanness. To know that is to enter the stable at Bethlehem and assist at the birth of the God of love – as my friend had done. And now when she looks into the beautiful face of her gloriously alive daughter all grown up and fearlessly encountering the world, she remembers that sunlit day in East Africa when she found the Christmas she thought she had lost.

An early Easter for Joe

Joe always loved Easter; it was his favourite time of year. He was really my brother's friend; they ran and swam and climbed together, two long-legged powerhouses, always on the move, always charged with the energy of their next adventure. The wind would catch their excited voices and bear them back to me as I trotted over the fields behind them on my much shorter legs.

When my brother died suddenly in his teens, leaving me desolate, Joe took over my care and protection. I couldn't have had a more loving, more responsible surrogate brother.

Joe died recently after a long illness. His last weeks were a miraculous time of great peace and deep happiness as his life slowly pared itself back to its essence – and its essence was good: rich with memories of his life's beautiful heart of light and love. He had been a talented photographer; now images he had once captured with his camera enchanted his mind: the lovely woods around his home alight with the colours of autumn; laughing faces and blood-red sunsets; a golden blaze of daffodils pushing through unexpected snow. His wife said he smiled all the time and once, close to the end, he asked her if it was Easter. 'It feels like Easter,' he said.

With thee
O let me rise
As larks, harmoniously,
As sing this day thy victories:
Then shall the fall further the flight in me.

FROM 'EASTER WINGS' BY GEORGE HERBERT

It is only after the dark and sombre Holy Week that Easter Day can sing its own glory: the soul's triumph over death; the eternal springs of hope; a world new-washed with the tears of the enlightened.

When he first knew he was seriously ill, Joe went into the dark and came face to face with terror. He knew abandonment. He experienced, I know, an overwhelming sense of loneliness. The world he loved so much and had engaged with so creatively was receding from him; its colours were dimming. But even then, through that dark, desolate time, Joe knew he was in good company, the best, in fact. The Man of Sorrows who walks with all who cry out in the night was walking with Joe through the darkness, lifting the burden from him and shouldering it himself, leading him away from that abandoned place known only to the sick, towards the light of Easter Day.

Joe moved towards the light of Easter with a smile on his face, still marvelling at the great beauty of the world he was leaving and the many blessings he had been gifted with throughout his life. Easter came early for Joe this year.

The cup

Father, if it is possible, let this cup pass me by.
Nevertheless, let it be as you, not I, would have it.

MATTHEW 26:39

Who is it that does not flinch in the face of oncoming pain?
Which heart, shrinking from impending travail, does not
echo with Christ's words?

I found myself travelling with another woman recently; we
were strangers to one another, but sometimes that sense of
being encapsulated in space with another person has the
effect of dissolving or, perhaps, ignoring, barriers that
might, in more ordinary circumstances, intrude themselves
and inhibit all but the most superficial communication.

My companion spoke movingly about her second chance at
happiness with a wonderful man: a kind, intelligent man,
her *anam cara*, her soul mate; a man, she felt sure, with
whom she was destined to find fulfilment and healing. And
now, after only travelling a little way on what she had hoped
would be a lifetime's journey together, he was terminally ill.
Her face was full of pain as she described her dread of what
lay ahead. She spoke of her struggle to hold on to her job as
well as take care of her beloved, whose wish to remain at

home until the end she was determined to respect; she spoke of her bone-aching weariness at the end of each day and of her dread that she would not be able to go on, that her strength would not hold out, that her courage would fail. But I know with certainty, with absolute conviction, that she will travel steadfastly on that hard road ahead and that it is her extraordinary capacity for love that will shine the light to guide her and keep her safe. It was a privilege for me to hold that strangers hand; it was a privilege to feel blessed by her courage, her reflection of the Divine. My prayer for her is that she may one day, to her enrichment, be able to hold her beloved close within her being: his life, his death, their love.

The courage of men and women who accept and drink the cup of suffering, however timidly, however fearfully, is a testament, I believe, to the presence of the Divine in each of us; and that courage is there for us to witness every day both within the compass of our own lives and the lives of strangers.

The longer I live, the more I marvel at the power of love, because it is always love that urges the trembling hand to reach out towards the cup, just as it was love that, two thousand years ago, moved the Man of Sorrows to reach out and accept his cup.

From darkness to dawn

'Could you not watch one hour with me?' The dawn, Jesus knew, which for others would banish the darkness with light and birdsong and flower-scented breezes, for him would only serve to mock the agony ahead. But now it was still dark and his soul cried out for the touch of another's hand on his, the voice of another to break the silence with rough male warmth. But his companions slept; Jesus waited alone.

There is a world between those who are sleeping peacefully and those whose eyes are dry with wakefulness, whose hearts are too leaden, too burdened, to find rest. Jesus walked on that lonely shore on the edge of the world where there is no sleeping. His quiet words to his disciples reach down through the ages to touch our hearts with a shared humanity: 'Could you not watch one hour with me?'

We turn to the east and long for the dawn, but the darkness engulfs us. Our cries are lost in the darkness that seems to deny the dawn; the darkness that seems to deny our longing for the light to break over our heavy hearts and connect us once more to hope.

A voice reaches us from the seventeeth century, the voice of the religious poet, George Herbert, who articulates

the lonely cry of the soul lost in darkness in his poem,
'Deniall':

> When my devotions could not pierce
> Thy silent eares;
> Then was my heart broken, as was my verse:
> My breast was full of fears
> And disorder.
>
> My bent thoughts, like a brittle bow,
> Did flie asunder;
> Each took his way; some would to pleasures go,
> Some to warres and thunder
> Of alarms.
>
> As good go any where, they say,
> As to benumme
> Both knees and heart, in crying night and day,
> Come, come, my God, O come,
> But no hearing,
>
> O that thou shouldst give dust a tongue
> To crie to thee,
> And then not heare it crying! all day long
> My heart was in my knee,
> But no hearing.
>
> Therefore my soul lay out of sight,
> Untun'd, unstrung;
> My feeble spirit, unable to look right,
> Like a nipt blossome, hung
> Discontented.

O cheer and tune my heartlesse breast,
Deferre no time;
That so thy favours granting my request,
They and my mind may chime,
And mend my ryme.

In the beautiful prayer that constitutes the final verse of his poem, Herbert bears witness to the dawn. Harmony has been restored.

It is fear that renders us blind and deaf; panic and doubt that cause us to writhe impotently in the dark. Herbert receives the gift of the dawn and is restored to himself. He can hear again the quiet breath of God and he knows that he has never been abandoned. God has never once lost sight of him; it is he who has lost sight of God.

My mother was dying in the west of Ireland. The long, evening shadows darkened her room in the nursing home. She lay in a coma breathing calmly. I knew she could hear me and I talked to her about old times; about the life and the fun and the pain we had shared when I was growing up and afterwards. I told her again I was sorry for any hurt I had caused her.

The night was looking in at me so I drew the curtains together. I had lit some candles earlier and sat now in their quiet glow. My mother had often talked about the ceremony of lighting the lamps when she was a girl; she had loved the soft bloom of light they shed that, my father used to add, 'left the corners in decent darkness'. I knew she would appreciate the lit candles now. I thought of my ailing father lying, probably sleepless, in his bed at home. I suddenly felt very alone. I had told my husband there was no need to travel from our home in Derry until the following day. I was sorry now. I needed his solid presence near me. I was conscious of having no brothers or sisters. The full reality hit me and with a sickening lurch, I was free-falling in space, in darkness. I cried out for help.

And the door to my mother's room opened. Two figures came in quietly, followed by a third – and a fourth. Women. Relatives – and friends. They embraced me in silence, holding me in the circle of their arms. An hour later I said, 'Look at the time. You must go. You'll be exhausted tomorrow.' 'No, no,' they said, 'we're staying with you.' And they did. Right through the night. We talked. We reminisced. We wept. They shared their memories of my mother with me. We spoke of her generosity, her sharp wit, her unerring ability to spot the third-rate from a mile off. Do you remember? Do you remember? And we did. We remembered it all. We wove my mother's life as we knew it into a tale of many beautiful colours. All through the night.

And when the dawn came, I felt I had never seen anything more beautiful: a dawn of dazzling light; of glorious resurrection; the dawn of the day my mother's spirit winged its way home.

And the darkness is befriended,
And we welcome the dawn.

Wait here and keep awake with me

'He took Peter and the two sons of Zebedee with him. And sadness came over him, and great distress. Then he said to them: "My soul is sorrowful to the point of death. Wait here and keep awake with me."'

Christ's words, issuing from the profoundest depths of desolation, show him at his most human. His words link him forever with our human condition of suffering, with the incurable loneliness of the soul in pain. 'My soul is sorrowful to the point of death.' The bleak landscape that gives birth to these words is one that is familiar to us. Those of us mourning our losses drag ourselves through its stark mid-winter fields where consolation comes to die and grief is rendered mute.

Love fails; we fail; the world appals; a child's reproachful eyes stare out of the screen at us; the depth to which we are consigned by our own stupidity threatens to overwhelm us and we are walking through that landscape again, that dark mid-winter field bisected raggedly by stunted, shivering blackthorns. Like a small, inconsolable child, riven through with the bleakest sense of loss, we are sorrowful to the point of death. But our eyes can be so blinded by tears that we fail to see that other figure walking beside us through the riven landscape.

As the rain hides the stars, as the autumn mist hides the hills, as the clouds veil the blue of the sky, so the dark happenings of my lot hide the shining of Thy face from me. Yet if I, man, hold Thy hand in the darkness, it is enough. Since I know, that though I, man, stumble in my going, Thou dost not fall.

FROM 'THE HEBRIDEAN ALTARS' BY ALISTAIR MACLEAN

'Wait here and keep awake with me.' Throughout the night, two women, an older and a younger, walk the youngers' sick and fretful child up and down, up and down the length of the silent room; cold ashes in the grate; a blue, one-eared rabbit discarded on the floor. Up and down, up and down, shushing, soothing. The younger woman's face is strained and white, her eyes are wide and frightened. From time to time sounds of sleeping from other parts of the house punctuate the dark hours. The older woman takes the child from his exhausted mother and walks him up and down, up and down, soothing his small whimpering moans, murmuring endearments into his hot, damp neck, humming a lullaby from long ago. The woman's arms ache and burn with the weight of the sick child. The older woman urges the younger one to sit and rest, to drink the tea she's made for her, and she holds her arms out for the child again.

In the grate she's set and lit a fire and flames are licking upwards. 'Look!' she whispers to the child, 'look at the pretty dancing flames,' and the child smiles a tiny smile before his eyes swoon and close in blessed sleep. The long night is over. The child is sleeping peacefully in his cot. The women sit close together looking into the fire and weave a prayer of gratitude out of their weariness.

'Wait here and keep awake with me.' With these words spoken to his friends, Jesus enshrined friendship in sacredness forever.

Friendship drops into the heart of one's life like a sudden gift. Someone once said there is a mother's heart in the heart of God, and it is a mother's desire for her child to have a true friend who will shine a good light for him; who will know when he is in need of consolation and who will stay awake with him through the long night when he can find no rest.

It was the mother's heart in the heart of God which gave the Son of God the consolation of the warm, breathing presence of friends throughout the dark night of the soul. Yes, they slept, but their flawed humanity caused them to be no less beloved by their Master. His human need for his friends' company and their all too human heavy-lidded response together wove an everlasting sheltering cloak for us all.

In the darkness of the evening
the eyes of my heart are awake to you.
In the quiet of the night
I long to hear again intimations of your love.
In the sufferings of the world
and the struggles of my life
I seek upon your graces of healing.
At the heart of the brokenness around me
And in the hidden depths of my own soul
I seek your touch of healing, O God
for there you reside,
In the hidden depths of life, O God,
There you reside.

'A hospital ward at 4 o'clock in the morning is the loneliest place in the world,' a mother in mourning for her child wrote recently. And it is. I know. You know. But the cold, bleak landscape of the hospital ward is not empty; there is a presence dimly seen through veils of tears that has shared the hours of darkness and sorrow with you and that will stay with you until the morning of your healing dawns.

A man breaks free from the grip of a terrifying nightmare and sits up in bed choking and gasping with sobs – only to face again the sickening realisation that the nightmare is his waking reality. 'How can I get through this on my own?' he weeps. He is not alone. His hours of darkness have been shared already. Already he is being lifted out of the depths and is being placed on firm ground. The consolation of Christ is all around us and all through us. And although we may not be able to pray, prayer is all about us and all through us. Carol Ann Duffy's beautiful poem conveys this movingly:

Prayer Finisterre
Some days, although we cannot pray, a prayer
utters itself. So, a woman will lift
her head from the sieve of her hands and stare
at the minims sung by a tree, a sudden gift.
Some nights, although we are faithless, the truth
enters our hearts, that small familiar pain;
then a man will stand stock-still, hearing his youth
in the distant Latin chanting of a train.
Pray for us now. Grade 1 piano scales
console the lodger looking out across
a Midlands town. Then dusk, and someone calls
a child's name as though they named their loss.
Darkness outside. Inside, the radio's prayer –
Rockall. Malin. Dogger. Finisterre.

At the heart of silence

For someone who is wedded to the spoken and written word, someone whose professional life is spent exploring and explaining words – and whose private life rarely sees her leaving words aside – my most profound experiences almost always have been at the heart of silence. And as I get older my longing for times of silence grows apace with my intolerance for gratuitous noise. As humans we are expert in erecting walls of words, cacophonous barriers against the silence that holds the truths from which we wish to hide. I know because I've built many a wall myself with the ready help of shouts, arguments, jokes and jingles.

It isn't at all that I have fallen out of love with the gift of language – far from it; it is that my growing appreciation for the gift of silence means that I lend a more critical ear to that which breaks it. Truth, beauty, silence, I have discovered, live harmoniously together.

Once, sitting alone on a rocky outcrop in Donegal, gazing out at the grey-green Atlantic; once in a little old twelfth-century church deep in a wood in France, I gave myself up to the power of silence, experienced the warm assurance of a loving Creator and felt a happiness unparalleled in its completeness.

When I was a child spending long summers on my grandparents' farm, I remember flying through the moon-drenched fields on my way back from playing with my holiday friend, flame-haired Sal, late again for family night prayers. Just as I reached the stile, which gave access to the apple-garden, light-headed with the smell of wild honeysuckle from the hedges, I stopped, gazed back into the silent moonlit fields, and my soul wept with the knowledge of love.

Recently, I stepped into my garden very early on a late September morning, a mellow morning veiled in warm mists. Shrubs were laced in delicate cobwebs; dew wept on late roses. The silence was unbroken. The sun broke through mists, the light glinted and glittered, gathering up the colours of the garden. Involuntarily, I smelt again the intoxicating scent of wild honeysuckle and ripe apples, stood barefoot in the hushed, moon-drenched fields, and knew again the God of love at the heart of silence.

And then, someone within turned on the radio, unleashing voices speaking of dissension and disagreement, wars and rumours of war. Just the news. If you listened carefully you could hear the sound of walls being built, brick on brick.